Leckie×Leckie
Scotland's leading educational publishers

SECOND EDITION
2

HIGHER
History
course notes book 1

✕ John A Kerr ✕

Text © 2010 John Kerr
Design and layout © 2010 Leckie & Leckie
Cover image © Getty Images

02/280311

ISBN 978-1-84372- 697-5

Published by
Leckie & Leckie Ltd
An imprint of HarperCollins*Publishers*
Westerhill Road, Bishopbriggs, Glasgow, G64 2QT
T: 0844 576 8126   F: 0844 576 8131
leckieandleckie@harpercollins.co.uk   www.leckieandleckie.co.uk

Special thanks to
Donna Cole (copy-edit),
Letts and Lonsdale (creative packaging)

The cover image shows armoury workers drinking milk to counteract the effects of their exposure to lead in the atmosphere of their factory.
(Photo by Fred Horley / Fox Photos / Getty images)

Mixed Sources
Product group from well-managed forests and other controlled sources
www.fsc.org Cert no. SW-COC-001806
© 1996 Forest Stewardship Council

FSC is a non-profit international organisation established to promote the responsible management of the world's forests. Products carrying the FSC label are independently certified to assure consumers that they come from forests that are managed to meet the social, economic and ecological needs of present and future generations.

Find out more about HarperCollins and the environment at
www.harpercollins.co.uk/green

Higher History has had a facelift by the SQA with several changes to old topics and some completely new topics added. This book focuses on Paper 1 in the Later Modern History option. If you are learning about Britain from the 1850s to 1951, or Germany between the years 1815 and 1939, then this book is for you.

Each topic in the new Higher History syllabus is divided into six issues and usually each chapter will focus on a separate issue.

Each issue starts with 'The big picture', which gives an overview of what the issue is about.

Getting the best results possible

Paper 1 of your Higher History exam will be assessed by essays. You will have 80 minutes to complete two essay questions, and it is vital you know how to write essays in order to be successful in the exam. Leckie & Leckie's Higher History Grade Booster will give advice about the process of writing essays, but you should also know about the way your essays will be marked.

Each essay is marked out of 20. These 20 marks will be made up of three parts: knowledge, structure and analysis.

Knowledge

You must have at least six different pieces of detailed relevant information because you can get up to six marks for **knowledge**.

How do I score knowledge marks?
You will score marks each time you use a correct and relevant piece of information to support a main point. You will get a second mark if you develop that information point further. However you will not get a mark for every piece of information you include.

Supposing you wrote, "The Liberals passed many social reforms one of which was Old Age Pensions. In 1908 Lloyd George introduced the Old Age Pensions Act that provided between 1 shilling and 5 shillings a week to people over seventy. These pensions were only paid to citizens on incomes that were not over 12 shillings. The pensions were only paid to people of good character who had not been in prison for the previous 10 years."

This paragraph has at least seven hard facts in it. Clearly it would be unfair to give 6 out of 6 knowledge points just on pensions. So no matter how much you write on PART of your answer you will only score at most 2 points for KU.

Structure

You will also gain up to four marks for **structure**. Structure means you must have a clear introduction, a middle section of several paragraphs where you develop your ideas by showing off what you know, and then a conclusion. You will not get any knowledge and understanding (KU) marks within your introduction so keep to the point. There is much more advice on introductions and conclusions throughout this book.

Analysis

Finally there are 10 marks (half your total) where you must use your information to answer the question asked. You must show you have understood the question and are using your information and ideas to answer the question directly. It's never enough just to tell a story!

Britain
1850 – 1951

Introduction

The first part of this book deals with Britain from the 1850s to 1951 and the six issues are:

Issue 1 – Why did Britain become more democratic between 1867 and 1928?

Between 1850 and 1928 Britain underwent great social and political changes that resulted in it becoming more democratic. You should aim to find out the reasons why political change happened and WHY Britain became more democratic between the 1860s and 1918.

Issue 2 – In what ways did Britain become more democratic between 1867 and 1928?

You should be able to describe what a democracy means and in what ways political changes in Britain made Britain more democratic between 1867 and 1928.

Issue 3 – Why did women in Britain gain greater political equality by 1928?

In 1850, women were seen as 'second class citizens'. They had no vote and most were denied access to education or well-paid jobs. By 1918 some women were given the vote for the first time and by 1928 women over 21 gained the vote on the same terms as men. What had caused such changes?

Issue 4 – Why did the Liberal government of the early 20th century become involved in passing social reforms?

Attitudes about what the government should do to help people began to change. By the early 1900s a realisation grew that poverty had causes which were often beyond the control of any one person to solve. However there were several other influences at work that persuaded the government to take action to ease the problem of poverty. What were those influences?

Issue 5 – How effectively did the Liberal reforms deal with the problem of poverty in early 20th century Britain?

Between 1906 and 1914 the Liberal governments introduced a series of reforms that tried to help the young, the sick, the old and the unemployed. How far did these reforms help the deserving poor?

Issue 6 – How successful was the Labour Government of 1945–51 in dealing with the social problems facing Britain after World War Two?

The Labour government of 1945–51 put into operation a Welfare State in which the government took responsibility for the wellbeing of its citizens and provided a safety net through which nobody should fall into poverty. But how successfully did the Labour Government deal with the social problems facing Britain after World War Two?

Issue 1 – Why did Britain become more democratic between 1867 and 1928?

> ## The big picture
> This issue really focuses on the pressures that caused Britain to become more democratic. Because this issue starts in 1867 and ends in 1928 – two significant dates for voting rights – this chapter looks mainly at the reasons for giving more people the right to vote, also known as franchise reform.
>
> Each reform of the franchise was the result of different pressures and it is only in hindsight that we see an apparently linked sequence of reforms that extended the franchise in Britain. This section looks at the pressures that caused those changes.

Economic and social change as pressures for reform

During the 19th century and early 20th century there were huge social and economic changes happening in Britain. These changes did not cause any one reform but were part of changes sweeping across Britain that led to pressure for change and then change itself. A new word to consider is **overarching**. Like an arch that reaches over many things, overarching reasons are those that led to many changes. These social and economic overarching reasons can also be called long-term reasons for change. For example, changes in the British population (called demographic change) had effects on the political system right through the 19th century. The changes such as urbanisation (growing size of towns) did not immediately cause political change but led to the pressures for change.

On the other hand, short-term change is much more directly linked to cause and effect. In other words, because something happened then a political change happened soon afterwards that was directly caused by the first change.

Some of the reasons for change are shown in the following diagrams.

The effects of the Industrial Revolution

Long-term issues affecting the franchise

Changing Political Attitudes

The industrial revolution changed the way people worked, where they lived, how they travelled around the country and even how they felt about their position in society. The next diagram shows some of the changes linked to the industrial revolution and later these points will be more fully developed.

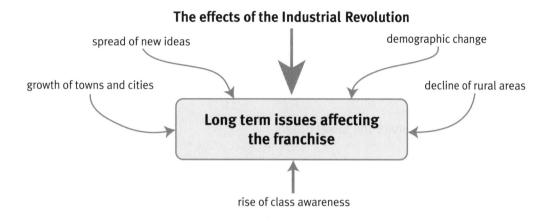

The effects of the Industrial Revolution

spread of new ideas

growth of towns and cities

demographic change

decline of rural areas

Long term issues affecting the franchise

rise of class awareness

Long-term pressures for change

The effect of a changing population
Demographic change means changes in the British population. Not only did the population grow but also the population distribution changed. That means where people lived changed and the main change is that more and more people left rural areas and moved into towns. By the 1850s, for the first time ever, the population in towns in England equalled the population in the countryside. In Scotland the change was slower but by 1900 migration from the Borders and the Highlands and Islands to the central belt had created the same situation. By 1950 Scotland's urban population was far bigger than its rural population.

The effect of the industrial revolution
For hundreds of years political power was in the hands of people who owned vast areas of the land of Britain. They were the most wealthy and most powerful people in Britain. The industrial revolution changed that. The new wealth lay with factory owners, mine owners and those involved in trade and business. The wealthy middle class now wanted a say in the running of the country. They argued that because they were the new wealth creators of the country they should have more of a say in the running of the country.

More effects of urbanisation and industrialisation
Another pressure for change caused by urbanisation and industrialisation (work based more in huge factories and mines) was the growing class awareness of the working classes. They realised that they too were wealth creators yet had no power at all to change anything. Yet in cities the working classes saw thousands of people in the same situation as themselves. Perhaps, if they united, change could be achieved.

You will find out about the Reform Acts of 1867 and 1884 and also touch on the First Reform Act of 1832. The link between social and economic change and these reforms is that in 1832 greater influence was given to the middle class and by 1867 the vote was given to the skilled working class in towns. In 1884 rural workers were included. These changes all show the drift of power to urban industrial Britain – the long-term overarching reasons were having an effect.

The social and economic changes in 19th century Britain also had an effect on the power of the land-owning rich. Put simply, their power declined. Other changes such as the Secret Ballot took away the power of old authority to bully the new voters while the redistribution of seats in 1867, 1885 and 1918 recognised that political power now lay with the people of Britain and the majority lived in towns. The old fashioned idea that land owners should rule Britain simply because they owned the land had died by 1900.

Short-term reasons for change

The 1867 Reform Act – in any answer about franchise reform you must also be able to deal with the more immediate short-term reasons for change. Historians tend to identify several short-term reasons for the 1867 Second Reform Act, some more important than others.

These reasons are:
- growing support for new ideologies
- political advantage
- political inevitability
- the effect of war
- pressure groups
- increasing respectability of the lower orders.

Reason 1 – Growing support for new ideologies

By the mid 19th century political ideas of Liberalism (the right of individuals to express their opinions freely) and democracy (the right of adults to choose the governments that ruled them) were becoming more widespread and accepted. In the USA and in Europe struggles were taking place for liberty and a greater political say for 'the people'. Britain tended to support these moves elsewhere so how could the British government continue to block these ideas in Britain?

Reason 2 – The growing respectability of urban artisans

Politicians were not so concerned with the danger of revolution breaking out as they had been earlier in the century. The old middle and landowning class belief that the 'working classes' could become an unthinking violent mob was ending. The fear that exploded across Europe among the old rulers of Europe at the time of the French Revolution of 1789 was now over 70 years old. By the 1860s skilled working men in cities (called artisans) were more educated and respectable. They attended night schools, took part in local politics and were concerned with improving their living standards.

Education Acts in the early 1870s in England and Scotland meant that the working class population was becoming increasingly educated and literate. In the 1860s, when civil war raged in the USA some British textile workers even chose to accept wage cuts rather than work with cotton picked by slaves in the USA. Politicians in Britain believed the actions of the textile workers showed the working classes as thinking people having 'a moral conscience' who deserved the right to vote.

Reason 3 – National protest campaigns and pressure groups were sometimes effective and always gained publicity

The well-organised campaigns of the National Reform League and Reform Union are good examples of early pressure groups campaigning for political change. Other examples of pressure groups include trades unions, the early Labour Party and even the women's campaign for the vote. (You can find out more about the women's campaign later in this book). They were all groups who used various methods to put pressure on the government to make changes.

Reason 4 – Fear of violence if changes did not happen

Earlier in the 19th century there was a feeling that allowing some reform would reduce pressure for greater changes. Although fears of large scale revolution faded, demonstrations in Glasgow and riots after a large meeting in Hyde Park, London, in 1866 worried the authorities. Members of the Reform League marched to Hyde Park. They found the gates locked and some marchers tore down the railings and trampled the flower beds. The middle class had nightmares of revolution! Some reform would calm those fears.

Reason 5 – A political advantage for the party that passed reform?

This is probably the most important reason for the Second Reform Act. You'll probably read in other sources that the Conservatives wanted to 'dish the Whigs' by 'stealing the Liberal's clothes'. What does that mean? Quite simply, Benjamin Disraeli, the leader of the Conservative Party in the House of Commons, believed that if his party gave the vote to working class men in the towns then these men would vote Conservative in future. When the Liberal government collapsed over the issue of how much reform to give, Disraeli saw his chance. In 1867 the Conservative party stole many of the Liberals ideas ('stole their clothes') and spoiled their chances of winning support from working class men. An old-fashioned word for spoiling something is 'to dish it' and an old name for the Liberals was 'Whig' – so that's why 'dish the Whigs' is used when referring to 1867 Reform Act.

Reason 6 – Objection to change lessened as time passed so further change became inevitable

It is often the case that after an event that has been fought over for so long eventually happens then the fears of those who were against the change simply vanish. Such was the case with the Third Reform Act. Although it was still 16 years after the previous reform, other changes in the political system such as the Secret Ballot Act and the Corrupt and Illegal Practices Act had continued the path to democracy and a fairer political system. In that situation it was almost inevitable that there were many voices declaring that the different voting rules between countryside (county) and town (boroughs/burghs) seemed pointless. There now seemed little difference between urban and rural workers, so the Reform Act removed the distinction.

Certainly the changing urban/rural balance in Britain meant that the power of the land-owning aristocracy was declining by the 1880s. City-based politicians resented the power of the old land-owning class, especially now that almost half the population was living in towns. Because voting was made secret in 1872, the city MPs hoped rural working men would vote for who they wanted – not necessarily the landowners. That would weaken the power of the old land-owning families in Parliament. Pressure for reform grew.

The same idea of inevitable change was also a reason for women finally winning equal political rights with men. The issue of votes for women had split the country before the Great War and even in 1918 there were concerns over the consequences of votes for women. However, ten years later there was hardly one voice raised against the granting of votes for women at the age of 21 on the same basis as men. The principle of votes for women had long since been accepted and no longer was a source of argument.

Reason 7 – Socialism might grow as a bigger threat if no change was allowed

In the later 19th century a new ideology was growing among the working classes. It was called socialism. At its simplest, socialists believed that working people produced the wealth of the country yet they lived in the worst conditions and were paid low wages. Socialists wanted to change the way the country was run and take wealth away from the rich and use it to make life better for the working classes. In other countries, socialists were involved in revolutions. In Britain it was argued that if large numbers of working people were denied the vote they might be attracted to revolutionary socialism. Socialism was seen as a threat by both landowners and businessmen. By allowing more working people the right to vote, it was thought they might be less likely to support revolutionary socialist ideas.

Reason 8 – The Great War was a catalyst that made change happen more quickly

This reason can only apply to the 1918 Reform Act. Nevertheless it is vital to include this in any answer to a question asking about why political change happened between 1867 and 1918.

Be careful with this section. Many of the reasons outlined here could become long and complex and take up a lot of your time. Be realistic.

Many candidates argue that women replaced men on the home front during the war, and were given the vote as a 'thank you' in 1919. That's far too simple and its only part of the changes that took place in 1918. See also issue 3 on Votes for Women. Try to expand your answer on the importance of the war to other areas.

One of the key rules about who could vote involved a residency qualification that meant you had to have lived at the same address for some time. Men who were away fighting had lost that qualification. It was politically unacceptable to tell those men when they returned from the war that they had lost their right to vote so the rules had to change.

In 1916, conscription was introduced for the first time in Britain. Men were ordered to join the armed forces or do work of national importance. Was it right that the government could order men to fight and kill on its behalf and not allow these men a chance to choose the government? That's why when the election was finally held in 1919, all men who had been in the armed forces were allowed to vote at 19 and would not have to wait until they were 21.

During the war, Lloyd-George, who was more willing to accept change, replaced Prime Minister Asquith, who was against votes for women.

By 1917–18 there were plans to change the rules about voting as they applied to men, and as the rules were changing anyway it was suggested that some women could also be included.
Finally, don't ignore the point about women doing men's jobs and keeping the home front going during the war. Undoubtedly, the sight of women 'doing their bit' for the war effort gained them respect and balanced the negative publicity of the Suffragette campaign.

Thematic or chronological?

You now have a lot of information about why Britain became more democratic.

It would be possible to explain why Britain became more democratic by dealing with the reasons for each reform act in **chronological** order but so often the reasons, especially the long-term reasons, do not fit neatly into any one particular reform. That is why the information here is presented in a **thematic** way affecting the moves to reform generally. It is up to you to decide which way best suits the question you are answering.

Section summary
In this issue you should have learned that:
Issue 1 will ask about why the changes happened so you must know the reasons for change.
There were both short-term and long-term reasons to explain change. Both should be dealt with in an answer.
You should be prepared to deal with the franchise reforms of 1867, 1884, 1918 and 1928.

Practise your skills

This section shows you how to plan an essay based on the question:

What factors influenced the extension of the franchise up to 1918?

Remember – topic and task!

Decide what the question is about (the topic): why did more people get the right to vote between 1867 and 1918.

Decide what you have to do (the task). Show that you know that more people did get the right to vote and when the reforms happened:

- Take each of the reforms in turn and explain why they happened.
- Show that you are aware that the reforms also happened because of larger social changes throughout 19th and early 20th century Britain.

Essay advice

The beginning

The beginning or introduction must:

- Make it clear that you understand what the question is asking you to do.
- Outline the main ideas or arguments that you will develop or explain in the middle section of the essay.

Below is a possible introduction to show you how it's done. Once again there are six numbered points. Remember, it's a good tip to faintly number your main ideas – that tells you how many separate middle section paragraphs there should be based on the main points you 'signposted' in the introduction.

> There were many reasons why the franchise was extended to more and more people in 1867, 1884 and 1918 (1). These reasons included trying to win advantages for a particular political party (2), changing attitudes towards the 'lower classes' (3) and the effect of the Great War (4), which acted as a catalyst and speeded up change.
>
> Probably the most important reason was the effects of the industrial revolution (5), which changed where people lived, how they worked and how they felt about their position in society. Finally, another important reason why the franchise was extended was the change in political ideology (6), which changed from believing the right to vote should only belong to people who owned the land of Britain to believing that the vote should be the right of all adult British citizens.

The middle

The middle part is the longest. It must have:

- several paragraphs
- a new paragraph for each new point or idea.

The numbered sections that follow suggest ways of developing the points made in the introduction. You would still have to include the precise factual details.

1. This point shows that you know when the reform acts were passed and it lets an examiner know that you intend to deal with why the reforms happened (which is what the question asks) rather than write down the terms of the act. Memorisation of the details of the reform acts is almost always a waste of time. You will not be asked to recite the terms of the acts.
2. This is a reference to the section in this revision unit that deals with 'stealing the Liberals clothes' and 'dishing the Whigs'.
3. In 1867 the urban, skilled, working-class man was educated and not a revolutionary – so why not admit him to the political system by granting him the vote? In 1884 the same was true of other men in the countryside and in towns. If they were not admitted they might turn to the new ideology of socialism, which was seen as a threat. Let them into the system, after all they could only vote. Power in parliament was still in the hands of an educated and wealthy elite.

4. Don't forget to use the information about the 1918 reform act contained in the section on votes for women. It's vital!
5. This is an important point to make. Britain was changing very fast after 1850. Cities were growing and social classes were emerging. Large cities and factories housed thousands of people who suffered terrible working and living conditions. If they were not taken 'into' the system by giving them the vote, would they try to overthrow the system with revolution?
6. A key theme in this course is change in ideology. By 1918 there was a belief that parliament represented the people of Britain, not just the owners of land and property. After all the extension of the reform that year was called officially the Representation of the People Act.

Your conclusion

Finally you must have a conclusion. Your conclusion should answer the main question. It should sum up the points made and if possible suggest a debate between different ideas. In the case of this essay, use the contrast between long- and short-term reasons for change.

Summarise the short-term reasons and then consider the influence of the longer-term reasons. Finally end with your final decision – what do you think were the most influential reasons for change?

Start with, '*In conclusion ...*' and write one sentence that makes a general answer to the main question, such as, '*In conclusion there were both short- and long-term reasons for franchise reform up to 1918.*' Then write, '*On one hand ...*' and summarise your information that supports one point of view about the essay title, such as, '*On one hand, gaining political advantage or responding to pressure groups or even reacting to the pressures of war led to franchise changes.*'

Continue with, '*On the other hand ...*' and here you must sum up the evidence that gives a different point of view about the main question such as, '*On the other hand, long-term changes in terms of demography, urbanisation and industrialisation changed the political face of Britain, making franchise reform inevitable.*'

Finally write, '*Overall ...*' and then write an overall answer to the main question, perhaps including what you think is the most important point made that led you to your final overall answer, such as, '*Overall, perhaps the most important influence on franchise reform was changing ideology and the growing acceptance that democracy was a political system worth having, and that could only be achieved through franchise reform.*'

Issue 2 – In what ways Britain did become more democratic between 1867 and 1928?

> ## The big picture
> In Britain before 1867 most men and no women had any say in choosing their government. They had no right to vote. However by 1928 almost all adults in Britain who were aged 21 or older could vote, so by 1928 Britain seemed to have become a lot more democratic.
> A democracy is more than just having the right to vote. It's also about how the political system became fairer and became more representative of the British people, who in turn were better informed about the choices they had.

What follows is information you would use in an essay on the growth of democracy in Britain after 1867.

What is a democracy?

Here is an introduction to a question about how democratic Britain had become by the early 20th century. The introduction shows some of the points to consider in any democracy essay. This introduction **signposts** the main themes that will be developed later in the essay.

How far did Britain become more democratic between 1867 and 1918?

For any country to be called democratic certain conditions have to exist. First of all, adults should have the vote (1) but the right to vote did not in itself make Britain democratic. Between 1867 and 1918, other features in a democracy were created that included a fair system of voting (2), a choice of who to vote for (3) and access to information to make an informed choice (4). It should also be possible for adults to become MPs themselves (5) and parliament should be accountable to the voters (6). Between 1867 and 1918 most, but not all, of these conditions had been met fully so Britain was more of a democracy but not entirely democratic.

In the introduction you'll see there are six numbered points. Each of these points is a main part of any answer about the growth of democracy in Britain. So six numbered points means there should be six main paragraphs in your answer to the question.

Another way to plan out the main paragraph to be developed is to draw a spider diagram. In the 'body' of the spider write the main question: In what ways did Britain become more democratic between 1867 and 1918?

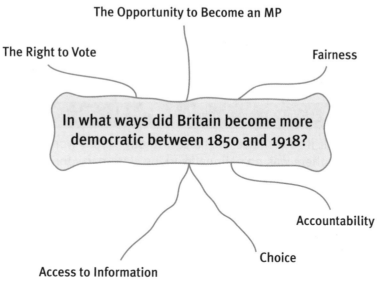

The Opportunity to Become an MP

The Right to Vote

Fairness

In what ways did Britain become more democratic between 1850 and 1918?

Accountability

Choice

Access to Information

Now you know that by using this diagram you can write the essay with six main paragraphs.

The following sections develop the headings in the diagrams and the points in your introduction. They provide detailed information to be added to your knowledge bank!

The right to vote

The right to vote was given to more and more people. This process was called the extension of the franchise. Without it the people of a country cannot influence political decisions.

This part of the course has a starting date of 1867. That is because a new law in that year gave the right to vote to most skilled working class men living in towns (also known as boroughs). By giving the vote to men owning property above a certain value and lodgers paying rent above £10 a year, the vote was extended to skilled working men who could afford to live in property above the required value. The effect of this reform nationally was to double the number of men who were entitled to vote.

The next extension of the franchise was 1884 when men living in the counties (generally it is ok to refer to counties as 'the countryside') were given the vote on the same rules as men in towns.

It took over 30 years more before the next franchise reform happened. In 1918 the Representation of the People Act gave the vote to another 13 million men and eight million women over 30 years of age. Not until 1928 did men and women aged 21 or over get equal political rights.

Fairness

In a democracy people should have a fair system of voting – and that meant two things had to happen if Britain was to become more democratic: voting in secret should be introduced and the distribution of MPs around the country would have to be rearranged. Corruption and threats had to be removed.

Although the 1867 Reform Act helped Britain become more democratic, voting was still open to bribery and intimidation. The Secret Ballot Act of 1872 allowed voters to vote in secret in polling booths and that certainly helped most intimidation and bribery.

The Corrupt and Illegal Practices Act 1883 limited how much candidates could spend during election time and banned activities such as the buying of food or drink for voters. Election expenses were limited and the intention was to make elections fairer with no political party dominating a constituency because of its wealth.

Another attempt to make the political system fairer was the redistribution of seats. Britain is divided into constituencies – areas of the country that send one MP to parliament. A constituency is also called a 'seat' because it represents one seat in parliament. In the mid 19th century the population spread across Britain had changed a lot. Towns grew in size while rural areas became less well populated.

The new laws in 1867, 1885 and again in 1918 tried to make the distribution of MPs across Britain fairer by giving the right to send more MPs to Parliament in busy areas and taking right to have an MP away from depopulated areas. This redistribution of MPs attempted to make political representation fairer, an important part of a democracy.

Choice

A country is not democratic if voters have no choice. Although many working class men had gained the right to vote in the 1880s there was no national working class party for them to vote for. However, by 1900 a new party – the Labour Party – had been created to campaign for working class interests. The development of the Labour party is most easily explained as a series of alliances between socialist groups and the realisation by trades unions that it would be helpful to have a political voice in parliament to look after the interests of the working classes. Not all working class men voted Labour of course but the creation of the Labour Party provided choice, an essential ingredient in a democratic society. However, for people to make a real choice they must have information about their candidates.

Access to information

Literacy is important in a democracy so that people can have access to information on which to base their choice. By the late 19th century, basic literacy was quite well established in Britain. The secret ballot and the extension of the franchise had also created a voting population eager for news and information. The development and spread of railways spread information quickly to all parts of the country while local authorities were convinced that improving people's minds and health were vital to a stable prosperous nation. In every town new libraries sprung up providing not only books but also newspapers and meeting rooms for debate and political meetings. Cheap daily newspapers also spread across the nation, carried by railways, while politicians used the rail network to criss-cross the country making speeches and building support.

Accountability means that parliament reflects the wishes of the voters and is answerable to them

In 1900, the House of Lords was not elected, yet it had power to scrap, or veto, any of the ideas of the elected MPs in the House of Commons. For Britain to be a democracy the power of the House of Lords would have to be changed. The issue came to a head when the Lords tried to block the right of the elected government to raise money through taxation. Without the money from taxes the government could not function. After a long argument and two more general elections the Parliament Act of 1911 resolved the situation. The Parliament Act of 1911 was an important step on the road to democracy in Britain. It reduced the power of the House of Lords, which now had no say over budgets and could no longer veto, or block, bills passed by the House of Commons. They could only delay them for two years.

The Parliament Act also reduced the maximum length of time between general elections from seven years to five and provided payment for Members of Parliament, thereby allowing men of the working class to consider standing for election as an MP.

The opportunity to become an MP

In a democracy, people who want to be involved in politics should be able to participate. That might mean joining a political party or standing for election as an MP. When political power was in the hands of wealthy landowners the issue of payment for MPs never arose. They felt it was their duty to serve their country. They were also wealthy enough to spend time in parliament without worrying about payment. For most of the 19th century, MPs were not paid and had to own land. Although the property qualification to become an MP ended in the 1850s, working class men, who had to work for their living for fairly low wages, could not afford to give up their day job to become a politician. Without regular payment how could they or their families survive?

For Britain to become more democratic the chance to become MP would have to be opened to everyone, and in 1911 the Parliament Act introduced payment for MPs, thereby allowing ordinary people greater access to the political process.

Section summary
In this section you should have learned that for a country to be democratic it is not enough just to give the vote to people. Lots of other conditions have got to be met. From 1867 onwards, the vote was given to more and more people but fairness, accountability, access to information with which to make informed choices and the right to participate directly in the political process, were all developments that carried Britain further towards democracy.

This section shows you how to plan an essay based on the question:

How far did Britain become more democratic between 1867 and 1918?

Remember – topic and task!

The first thing to do is to get a clear idea of what the topic (or subject) of the essay is about and also to decide what you need to do (the task) to answer the question fully.

This question is about the changes that took place between 1867 and 1918 which seemed to make Britain more democratic. That is the topic of this question. The task is to use your information to argue a case that Britain did become more democratic and to explain how the changes that took place helped the growth of democracy.

One of the first tasks for any essay preparation should be to find relevant information to include in the essay. To help you in this early essay look at the spider diagram below. You have seen a similar one before. This one uses all the main points needed but this time it also includes some of the detailed information needed. Feel free to add more detailed and relevant information.

The Opportunity to Become an MP
Abolition of property qualification for MPs, 1857
Payment for MPs, 1911

The Right to Vote
Second Reform Act, 1867
Third Reform Act, 1884
Representation of the People Act, 1918

Fairness
The Ballot Act, 1872
Redistribution of Seats Act, 1885
(and also in 1867 and 1918)
Corrupt and Illegal Practices Act, 1883

Did Britain become more democratic between 1850 and 1918?

Party Organisation
Conservative Central Office
Primrose League, 1881
National Liberal Federation, 1877
Branch Associations

Accountability
The Parliament Act, 1911
The loss of the House of Lords' veto

Access to Information
Education Act 1870 (1872 in Scotland)
Spread of railways from the 1850s
Cheap national newspapers

Choice
Three national parties to vote for
by the early 1900s

Essay advice

The beginning

The beginning or **introduction** must make clear that you understand what the question is asking you to do. Your introduction must also outline the main ideas or arguments you will develop or explain in the middle section of the essay.

Look back at the introduction to this essay that appeared earlier in this chapter. It had numbered points in it. To start your essay-writing skills use this introduction as your own. You can change it to suit your style later.

The middle

Once you have the introduction you must then start developing each main point, preferably in its own paragraph. This is the **middle** development part of the essay and is the longest.
It must have:

- several paragraphs
- a new paragraph for each new point or idea
- a key sentence to start each new paragraph that outlines what the paragraph will be about
- paragraphs that show off your knowledge about the subject – the detailed knowledge contained in the paragraph must be relevant to the key sentence
- a short, one sentence summary at the end of each paragraph that links to the main question.

Your conclusion

Finally you must have a **conclusion**. It should answer the main question. It should summarise the points that support one side of the argument. It should then sum up the arguments against the idea in the title. Finally, end with your final decision.

Start by writing, '*In conclusion* ...' and write one sentence that makes a general answer to the main question. Then write, '*On one hand...*' and summarise your information that supports one point of view about the essay title.

Then write, '*On the other hand...*' and here you must sum up the evidence that gives a different point of view about the main question.

Finally write, '*Overall...*' and then write an overall answer to the main question, perhaps including what you think is the most important point that led you to your final overall answer.

Here is an example:

> In conclusion, Britain did become more democratic between 1867 and 1918 but was not yet fully a democracy. On one hand, more people gained the right to vote, the system became fairer, there was more choice and people had access to information to make informed choices. On the other hand, women did not yet have full political equality with men. Overall, Britain was much more democratic than it had been in 1867 but still had some way to go, including even reforming the UK 'first past the post' voting system, which still raises criticisms.

You will see that proportional representation (PR) is alluded to. PR is a voting system that some people say makes for a fairer system. It is not vital to know about it in this course at all but it is here as an example of mentioning briefly a relevant point you know is useful and using it to support your balanced conclusion.

For more detailed advice about essay writing see *Leckie & Leckie's Higher History Grade Booster*.

Section summary

The idea of democracy in Britain had become well rooted by the later 19th century. The vote had been given to more people and a fairer, more accountable system had been created. Voters now had clear choices and could use the secret ballot to make sure they could vote for their own choice. The power of landowners and also the House of Lords had been reduced while the elected House of Commons had stronger powers to represent the electors of the country.

While some could argue that women did not have political quality with men, it was clear that progress was being made and further change was only a matter of time.

Overall, it is clear that by 1900 Britain had become much more democratic than it had been in the 1860s.

Issue 3 – Why did women in Britain gain greater political equality by 1928?

The big picture

Before 1918, women had no national political voice. They had no vote. In 1918 some women did gain the right to vote and in 1928 women gained political equality with men.

This issue looks at the reasons why women were given, or won, political equality. It also looks at the campaign for women's suffrage and asks just how effective the different protest methods were. There are many points that have to be considered when deciding why women gained greater political equality with men. The following diagram sums up the points you should know about.

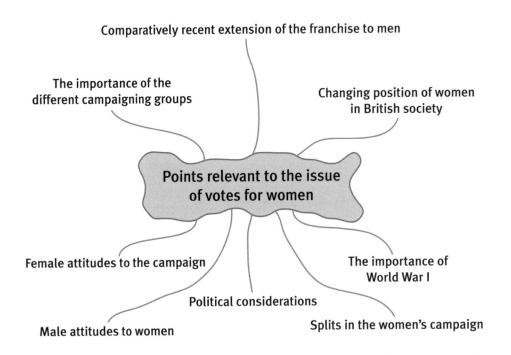

Comparatively recent extension of the franchise to men

The importance of the different campaigning groups

Changing position of women in British society

Points relevant to the issue of votes for women

Female attitudes to the campaign

The importance of World War I

Political considerations

Male attitudes to women

Splits in the women's campaign

Male attitudes

Social attitudes are very slow to change and many men still saw women as inferior. Women were often seen as irrational, emotional and not suited to politics! Politicians argued that women would simply vote as their husbands told them – or they would vote for the best looking candidate. But don't assume all men were against votes for women. In 1867, John Stuart Mill, MP, tried to get votes for some women included in the 1867 Reform Act. His suggestion was defeated but 73 men in parliament did support him.

Changing position of women in British society

Historian Martin Pugh argues that by 1900 the view that women should have no national political voice was 'untenable', which means it was very hard to justify not giving the vote to women. By 1900, women – especially middle class women – were better educated, often attended university, and could even vote in local politics. Women were also increasingly important in trades unions. Changes in the law had also improved women's social position.

So don't fall into the trap of saying in your exam that all women were second class citizens, treated as their husband's property, and just 'given away' by one man to another on their wedding day. That attitude was more common in 1850 but was changing by 1900. Changes around the world also had an effect. Other countries such as New Zealand had given the vote to women, so why not Britain?

Female attitudes to the campaign

Not all women supported votes for women. Queen Victoria famously described the women's suffrage campaign as, 'that mad wicked folly of women's rights'. When women's suffrage groups presented petitions to parliament in support of their demands for votes for women, it was relatively easy for politicians to ignore them because of the fairly low numbers of signatures.

The importance of the different campaigning groups

The role of the NUWSS

In 1897, a number of local women's suffrage societies formed the National Union of Women's Suffrage Societies (NUWSS). The NUWSS believed in peaceful tactics to win the vote, mainly for middle class property owning women. The NUWSS was nicknamed the 'Suffragists' but be careful when writing about them. Some historians have said the government took no notice of them but recent research suggests the NUWSS was important. Membership of the NUWSS remained high (53 000) members in 1914, and when the Suffragettes became more violent, membership of the NUWSS rocketed as women left that group.

The Suffragettes

In 1903 the Women's Social and Political Union (WSPU) was formed. Their motto was 'deeds not words' and at first they grabbed the headlines through large peaceful demonstrations, but from 1910 onwards the Suffragettes became more militant, which means that they used more violent protest methods.

Beware! Do not spend a long time just describing what the Suffragettes did. Use some examples to help answer the question set.

How important were the Suffragettes?

A point often made in exam answers is that the Suffragettes kept the issue of women's suffrage in the headlines. It is true that violent Suffragette methods such as firebombs, and attacking politicians, hunger strikes and the resulting Cat and Mouse Act made big headlines. But was all the publicity useful? Did it not just make the government determined to not give in to terrorism as it would be called today?

To illustrate the debate about the importance of the Suffragettes you could use historian Martin Pugh's argument, which mainly rejects the importance of the Suffragettes. He points out that:
- Suffragette membership fell while the membership of the NUWSS increased between 1910 and 1914.
- Suffragettes destroyed sympathy for the issue of votes for women among MPs who had previously supported it.
- When the question of giving votes to women was being debated seriously in 1917 the Suffragettes had long since stopped their campaign.
- The Suffragettes were a small group whose self publicity lasted longer than their real importance.

Another point to make about the Suffragettes is that they made serious planning mistakes. Mrs Pankhurst and her Suffragettes failed to link with the Labour Party to increase democracy in Britain. They ignored the thousands of working class men who still had no voice and Mrs Pankhurst was even willing to settle for granting the vote to some wealthy women rather than campaign for the vote for all adults. Mrs Pankhurst's policy lost the Suffragettes political allies.

Emmeline Pankhurst - most people associate her with winning the right to vote for women? Others say she pushed back the chances of winning the right to vote and eventually she was an irrelevance. What do you think?

Political pressure and political advantage

If you use this as part of the suffrage answer you must deal with it carefully. The points here should be used to explain why the government chose to avoid as far as possible the issue of votes for women before the First World War.

The Liberals had too much to do.

When the Liberals came to power in 1906, women were campaigning loudly for the vote. However there were many other pressures on government time and the issue of women's suffrage was not a top priority.

Opposition from the Prime Minister

In 1908 H.H. Asquith became Prime Minister. He was against votes for women.

Ireland was a greater concern to the government than votes for women

Before 1914, all of Ireland was part of the UK but groups in Ireland wanted to break away from the UK or at least have some self-governing powers. Tensions were increasing and by 1912 there was a strong possibility that civil war could break out in Ireland. This was a serious concern to the government.

At the general election of 1910 the Liberal majority in parliament was slashed and they needed help from the Irish Nationalist MPs in Parliament. These Irish MPs told Asquith to drop the idea of votes for women and make self government for Ireland a top priority. Asquith needed Irish support so he agreed. However, Asquith had already told the suffragettes that if he won the 1910 election he might consider women's suffrage. The Suffragettes felt they had been betrayed by the government and became more violent after 1910.

The importance of the Great War

This is another common topic that candidates write about. Once again, be careful with it. Many candidates argue that women replaced men on the home front during the war, and were given the vote as a 'thank you' in 1918. That's far too simple.

The women who worked hard and risked their lives in munitions factories were mostly single, and in their late teens or early 20s. The women who were given the vote were 'respectable' ladies, aged 30 or over who were property owners or married to property owners. So try to expand your answer on the importance of the war to other areas.

These 'other areas' can be found in the chapter dealing with Issue 1 – reasons why Britain became more democratic.

Just to remind you or to direct you to the correct sections, the main points to make here are:
- residency concerns
- the consequences of conscription
- Lloyd George replaced Asquith as Prime Minister
- reform of male voters
- women's war work

And finally, did it really take a long time for women to win the right to vote?

Even after the reform of 1884, almost 40% of men did not have the right to vote. Politicians were unwilling to give the vote to women while so many men still had no vote.

Organised campaigns for women's suffrage began in 1866 and women were given the vote on equal terms to men in 1928 – only 60 years later and only 10 years after many men gained the vote for the first time too. So it's possible to argue that as part of historical change it was not a very long time but, to those involved, it did seem like a long time.

If a question in the exam asks you to go up to 1928 in your answer don't worry about not writing too much detail about the time between 1918 and 1928. The vast bulk of your essay should deal with the years up to 1918.

In 1918 the Representation of the People Act gave the vote to another 13 million men and 8 million women. Although women under 30 – and many poor women over 30 – still did not have the vote, 10 years later they did.

Extending the vote to all women on the same basis as men was suggested in 1924. It was delayed by some political opposition but in 1928 women and men were given equal rights to vote. It had ceased to be a big issue.

Section summary

In this section you should have learned:

- why there was opposition to votes for women
- why votes for women was a greater possibility by the early 1900s
- the relative importance of the Suffragettes and Suffragists
- why the Great War was an important factor in winning political equality for women.

Practise your skills

This section shows you how to plan an essay based on the question:

Why did it take so long for women to gain the right to vote?

Remember – topic and task!

Decide what the question is about (the **topic**): the issue of votes for women.
Decide what you have to do (the **task**):

- Be able to use accurate and relevant detail.
- Introduce and develop the varied reasons why some women did not receive the vote until 1918.

Essay advice

For advice in writing essay refer back to previous 'practise your skills ' sections and also Leckie & Leckie's Grade Booster Higher History .
Any essay you write must have a beginning, a middle and an end.

The beginning

The beginning or **introduction** must:

- make clear that you understand what the question is asking you to do
- outline the main ideas or arguments you will develop or explain in the middle section of the essay.

Practise writing an introduction by putting into words the points shown in the diagram at the beginning of this revision section. Not all the points shown there are relevant to the "why did it take so long" part of the question but an important skill is adapting your information to make it relevant in some way.

The middle

The middle part is the longest.
It must have

- several paragraphs.
- a new paragraph for each new point or idea.
- accurate, relevant detail.

Use the information in this section to develop the points in your introduction you have selected as relevant.

Your conclusion

Start by writing, '*In conclusion* ...' and write one sentence that makes a general answer to the main question such as 'In conclusion there were several reasons why it took women so long to gain the right to vote.'

Then write, '*On one hand* ...' and summarise your information that supports one point of view about the essay title such as, '*Some historians argue that it was not until the women's movement raised awareness and gained publicity for the cause that votes for women became more likely.*'

Then write, '*On the other hand* ...' and here you must sum up the evidence that gives a different point of view about the main question, such as 'On the other hand longer term changes in the status of women plus the catalyst of the Great War finally brought the issue of votes for women to a conclusion.'

Finally write, '*Overall* ...' and then write an overall answer to the main question, perhaps including what you think is the most important point made which led you to your final overall answer, such as '*Overall it seems likely that votes for women would eventually have happened but the reform of 1918 owed its existence almost entirely to the pressures of the Great War.*'

Issue 4 – Why did the Liberal government of the early 20th century become involved in passing social reforms?

The big picture

By the end of the 19th century there was increasing evidence that poverty had causes that were often beyond the ability of individuals to help themselves. When the Liberal government came to power in 1906 they began a series of social reforms. This issue looks at the reasons why the Liberals intervened to help ease the problem of poverty.

To understand why the Liberal Reforms were so important, some background information is needed.

In the mid 19th century, most people accepted that poverty and hardship were not things the government could or should do anything about. Governments had tried to improve the worst living and working conditions with Factory and Mines acts, and Public Health acts were reactions to the devastating cholera outbreaks that were linked to poor sewerage and the lack of fresh water in cities.

However the government became involved in helping the poor it would cost money. That would mean taxes would have to go up. The middle classes would have to pay more tax yet the money would not be spent on them. Why should they help people who, it was believed, were too lazy to help themselves?

In his book *Self Help* Samuel Smiles wrote, 'Self help is the root of all genuine growth,' and Norman Pearson, another 19th century voice on the topic of poverty believed, that the poor were, 'made of inferior material ... and cannot be improved'.

The point is that most of the middle classes and the government believed that little or nothing could be done to ease the problem of poverty so why did the Liberals launch such a wide-ranging series of social reforms when they came to power in 1906? There must have been very persuasive reasons and those reasons form the core of this issue, investigating why the Liberal government of the early 20th century became involved in passing social reforms.

You will not be expected to decide on any one reason to explain the reforms. Instead you should be able to identify the most important reasons and explain them. As an introduction, the following diagram introduces the points you should make in any answer to a question on why the Liberal Reforms happened.

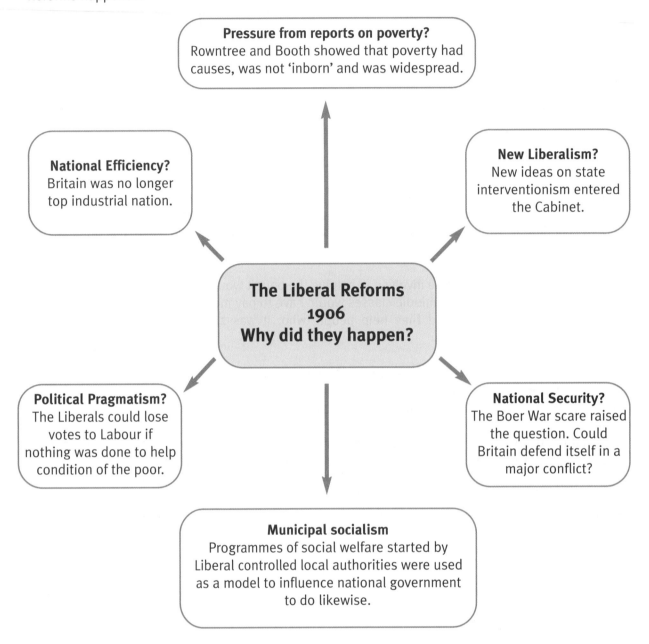

Pressure from reports on poverty?
Rowntree and Booth showed that poverty had causes, was not 'inborn' and was widespread.

National Efficiency?
Britain was no longer top industrial nation.

New Liberalism?
New ideas on state interventionism entered the Cabinet.

The Liberal Reforms 1906 Why did they happen?

Political Pragmatism?
The Liberals could lose votes to Labour if nothing was done to help condition of the poor.

National Security?
The Boer War scare raised the question. Could Britain defend itself in a major conflict?

Municipal socialism
Programmes of social welfare started by Liberal controlled local authorities were used as a model to influence national government to do likewise.

There is no one single reason to explain the Liberal reforms. In any answer you will be expected to consider all of the reasons. The following explanation of the various pressures on the government and reasons for change is not meant to suggest that one was more important than the other. They all influenced the Liberal government in some way.

Pressure on the government from reports on poverty

One of the most famous investigations into poverty was by Charles Booth. He carried out extensive research in London and presented his findings as hard, statistical facts, not opinions. He showed that poverty had causes, often beyond the control of the poor themselves. What could any individual do about low pay, unemployment, sickness and old age?

Another investigation into poverty in York was carried out by Seebawm Rowntree and was even more shocking. The Rowntree report showed that 30% of the York population lived in extreme poverty. People realised that if York, a relatively small English city, hid such problems then so would other British cities. The problem of poverty was therefore a national problem.

Worries about national security

When the Boer War started in 1899 volunteers rushed to join up – but almost 25% of them were rejected on the grounds that they were not fit enough. If men of military age were so unfit for service, the government worried about Britain's future ability to defend itself against a stronger enemy. The 1906 Report of the Inter-Departmental Committee on Medical Inspection and Feeding of Children attending Public Elementary Schools stated that there were very serious problems with children's health yet very little was being done about it.

Worries about national efficiency

By the end of the 19th century, Britain was no longer the strongest industrial nation and was facing serious competition from new industrial nations such as Germany. It was believed that if the health and educational standards of Britain's workers got worse, then the country's position as a strong industrial power would be threatened. In Germany a system of welfare benefits and old-age pensions had already been set up in the 1880s. If a main competitor could afford to do it why could Britain not do likewise?

The government felt that reforms might give them a political advantage

Many historians believe that the Liberal Reforms were passed for politically selfish reasons. Since 1884, most working class men had the vote and the Liberals wanted to attract those votes. But by 1906 a new party – the Labour Party – was competing for the same votes. If the Liberals were seen as unsympathetic to the poor, what might happen at elections in the future?

It was therefore to the political advantage of the Liberal government to offer social reform, even if they did not fully believe in the principle of government intervention in people's everyday lives.

The influence of New Liberal ideas

It would be far too harsh to argue that the Liberals passed social reforms just to win votes. A new generation of Liberal politicians genuinely believed that the government had a responsibility to help the poor.

The 'old Liberal' Prime Minister, Campbell Bannerman, died and was replaced by a younger man, Asquith, in 1908. New Liberals with new 'interventionist' ideas such as David Lloyd George were given important government jobs. The arrival into government of younger politicians with New Liberal ideas is the main reason why so many reforms happened from 1908 onwards.

The example of Municipal Socialism

Some Liberal-controlled local town councils became involved in improving the welfare of the people in their town. Local authorities that did try to tackle issues linked to poverty were used as a model to persuade national government that political intervention was both possible and desirable on a national scale.

Birmingham became an example of a local authority taking control of social services and utilities such as the water and gas supplies. In Glasgow, the town council also took control of the city water supply and provided street lighting along with many other municipal services. These services were paid for by local taxation. As the local taxes tended to be paid by the wealthy and were used to help the poor, the phrase 'municipal socialism' was used to mean local authorities spending money raised by local taxation for the public's benefit.

Increasingly, social reformers saw that the answer to poverty lay with the willingness of national government to tackle the national problem.

Section summary

In this section you should have learned the following:

- By the end of the 19th century there was increasing evidence that poverty had causes that were often beyond the ability of individuals to help themselves.
- There were various reasons why the Liberal government that came to power in 1906 started a programme of social reform. These included concern for the poor exposed in reports on poverty.
- There were worries about national efficiency and security.
- Political self-interest drove change.
- There was a growing political belief that governments should get more involved in social issues – if local government could do it why not national government?

Practise your skills

This section shows you how to plan an essay based on the question:

> To what extent did political advantage force the Liberals into a programme of social reform from 1906?

Every year some candidates lose lots of marks because they answer the 'wrong' Liberal Reform question. That means they write about why the reforms happened when the question really asks about the effectiveness of the reforms or vice versa.

It is therefore vital to sort out what a 'Liberal Reform' question is asking you to do. This example will help you to structure a relevant essay.

First of all think! And ask yourself what the question is about. At first you will see the **topic** words 'Liberals', 'social reform' and '1906' – it looks like it is about the Liberal Reforms, but it is not.

The essay title provides one possible explanation why the Liberal Reforms happened and you are asked if you agree with that view or should other reasons be considered. So the question is really about why the Liberal Reforms happened. You have to show your understanding of why political advantage influenced the Liberal decision to pass reforms and then decide if political advantage was the real reason why the Liberal Reforms happened or if other reasons were more important.

You should know there were other reasons apart from political advantage. This question asks 'to what extent' so you should be aware that you must demonstrate your knowledge about the other reasons and arrive eventually at a balanced conclusion.

Essay advice

Are there certain things that must be in an introduction?

Yes, it must have a sentence or two at most that sets the context of the reforms - for example a brief account of changing attitudes towards poverty. You must then have a sentence that suggests you are going to write a balanced essay by looking at all sides of the debate. You could do that by stating that political advantage was only one of many reasons. Then you should mention the other reasons but do not explain them yet. Remember this is your introduction.

Here is an example of a relevant introduction to this question:

By the early 20th century, most men, rich and poor, could vote. The new Labour Party promised social reform and the Liberals were worried about losing votes. Reform could therefore be seen as a rather selfish, political advantageous response to political change (1). The Liberal Reforms were also partly the result of concern for the poor, which had been highlighted by the reports of Booth and Rowntree which argued that 1/3 of Britain's population lived in poverty (2).

Other factors also played a part. The Liberals were concerned that Britain was losing its status as a major industrial and military power while concern over national efficiency and security played a part in the reforms (3, 4). Finally new attitudes in the Liberal Party, called New Liberalism (5) and Municipal Socialism (6) encouraged national government to consider greater intervention to help relieve poverty.'

Why is this a good introduction?

The style is mature and signposts clearly the points to be raised in the essay. It provides a structure which the candidate can follow through the rest of the exam. There is no irrelevance and it is clear to a marker you have understood the question.

Are there rules about what should be in a conclusion?

Yes. You must make your mind up and answer the main question. You should also sum up your main points. This can be a bit repetitive in that you will be mentioning the main points made in your introduction.

To make your conclusion effective and different, try to prioritise your reasons. This means you decide which of the many relevant points you raised in your introduction is the most important in the answer to the main question.

Never ever add more factual information into your conclusion. A conclusion ends your essay. It should not continue your essay or push it in a new direction by including new information.

What makes a good conclusion?

A conclusion should have four main stages:

- The first *stage* is the first sentence where you state your main answer.
- The second *stage* could start, '*On one hand* ...' and that introduces one side of your balanced conclusion.
- The third *stage* starts with '*On the other hand* ...' and here you present some evidence that balances or counters your earlier evidence.
- Your final *stage* is for weighing up your two arguments, and making your overall decision, perhaps starting with '*On balance* ...'

Here is an example to illustrate how this would look in reality:

In conclusion, the Liberal Reforms were the result of many influences. On one hand political advantage was an important factor in pushing the Liberals towards social reform. Fears of losing votes to the new Labour Party may have made the reforms a more pressing necessity. On the other hand, concern about Britain's position in the world made politicians realise that a healthier working class was necessary. Without the reports of Booth and Rowntree making people aware of dire poverty in Britain, perhaps the Liberals would not have responded with a programme of reforms. On balance, these reports made people realise that poverty was often beyond the individual's ability to help themselves and the concept of the deserving poor requiring assistance was at the core of the Liberal Reforms.

Issue 5 – How effectively did the Liberal reforms deal with the problem of poverty in early 20th century Britain?

> ## The big picture
> The Liberal Reforms of 1906–14 are very important because they marked the acceptance of the idea that the national government should have a large role in helping those who could not help themselves. Between 1906 and 1914 the Liberal Reforms tried to deal with the problem of poverty and focused on four groups: the old, the young, the sick and the unemployed.
>
> To answer a question dealing with this issue you will need to be able to do several things:
> * You should know accurate and detailed information about what the Liberal Reforms were.
> * Be able to explain what is meant by the problem of poverty. That means the problems which cause poverty, for example unemployment or old age, and also the problems caused by poverty such as bad health.
> * Link the problems of poverty to the reforms passed by the Liberals and decide whether or not the reforms helped solve the problems. In other words, decide how effectively the Liberal Reforms dealt with the problem of poverty in early 20th century Britain.

The Liberal Reforms 1906–14

There is no way to avoid learning what the Liberal reforms were. Start by organising the social reforms under four main categories – the old, the young, the sick, the unemployed. The following diagram should help you organise the basic information.

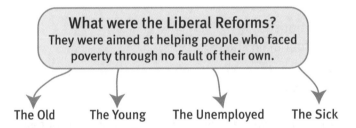

What were the Liberal Reforms?
They were aimed at helping people who faced poverty through no fault of their own.

The Old The Young The Unemployed The Sick

The old

What was done?
In 1908, the government started paying five shillings (25 pence) a week to people over 70. A married couple got 37·5 pence.

How effective was the reform?
Remember that Rowntree had set the poverty line for a single person at 35 pence, so the pensions would help the elderly poor but they were not the answer to old age poverty. In poorer areas of the cities, life expectancy was around 45 years so pensions at the age of 70 would help only very few of the poor who lived long enough to collect the pension. Most of the very poor died long before their 70th birthday. There were also some qualification rules that excluded some of the elderly. The pensions were a help, but certainly not a solution to old age poverty.

The young

What was done?
In 1906 free school meals were started for the poorest children. In 1907 school medical inspections started but it was not until 1912 that free medical treatment was available.

Social reformers blamed poverty for causing a lot of youth crime, so in 1908 juvenile courts and borstals – young people's prisons – were opened. It was believed that if young law breakers were sent to adult prison they would learn how to be better criminals.

All these reforms, including restricting the sale of cigarettes and alcohol to children, were called a 'Children's Charter' because it was believed this set of reforms would be like an old-fashioned document or charter that would guarantee better lives for children.

How effective were the reforms?

Researchers found that during school holidays the growth of poor children slowed and body-weight often declined. This suggests that school meals were an important part of the health of poor children.

Medical inspection did little to solve any problems so it was not until free medical treatment for school children was started that problems could be dealt with.

Early attempts to protect children from 'social evils' such as smoking and alcohol by setting minimum ages at which these things could be bought had limited success.

The sick

What was done?

There was no free National Health Service at that time. The poor could not usually afford medical help. The National Insurance Scheme of 1911 gave some medical benefits. The scheme was called a contributory system because each worker paid four pence a week towards the help they received. The employer paid three pence a week and the government paid two pence a week. That meant each insured worker got nine pence in benefits from an outlay of four pence. The plan was soon called 'ninepence for fourpence'. Everyone on low wages – up to £160 a year – was insured. An insured worker got ten shillings a week (50 pence) when off sick but the benefits only lasted for 26 weeks.

How effective were the reforms?

Illness and absence from work was the major cause of poverty, therefore any money coming in as 'sick pay insurance benefit' would help a family during hard times but only the insured worker got free medical treatment from a doctor. Other family members did not benefit from the scheme, no matter how sick they were.

The unemployed

William Beveridge, an advisor to Lloyd George said, 'The problem of unemployment lies at the root of most other social problems.'

What was done?

Labour exchanges were started that were similar to current-day job centres. Workers could find out easily what jobs were available in their area. You have already read about the National Insurance Act of 1911 earlier in this unit but the new law also dealt with unemployment. Like the health insurance reform, it was a combination of state help along with contributions from the worker.

Most insured workers got seven shillings (35 pence) a week for a maximum of 15 weeks.
Beware: the National Insurance scheme of 1911 applied both to health and unemployment. Although the part of the act that dealt with unemployment still involved contributions paid by workers, employers and the government it is not the famous 'ninepence for fourpence'.

How effective were the reforms?

The Act of 1911 was only meant to cover temporary unemployment and only applied to seven trades, most of which suffered seasonal unemployment. When long-term unemployment increased after the Great War the system started to fall apart, as the payments of those in work did not provide enough income for the government to pay out money to the unemployed.

Other reforms

In any question about the Liberal Reforms, look very closely at what specific area is being asked about. If the question asks about the Liberal Reforms in general you should remember that there were other reforms passed apart from the main ones mentioned here. These included:

- In 1908, miners secured an 8-hour day, the first time the length of the working day was fixed for adult men.
- In 1909, the Trade Boards Act tried to protect workers in 'sweat shops', such as tailoring and lace making by setting up trade boards to fix minimum wages and maximum hours.
- In 1911, the Shops Act gave shop assistants a weekly half day off.

How effective were the Liberal reforms?

In an answer to this you should think about what the reforms were meant to do. They were not meant to create a Welfare State. They were meant to provide some help to people who could be thought of as the deserving poor. Most of the reforms also depended on those who received help doing something to help themselves. The National Insurance Act is a good example of this idea. The government was prepared to intervene to help the poor, but as part of the deal the poor also had to help themselves by paying contributions towards their benefits.

Winston Churchill, then a Liberal MP, neatly summed-up the aim of the Liberal Reforms. He said, ' If we see a drowning man we do not drag him to the shore. Instead we provide help to allow him to swim ashore.' In other words, the Liberals tried to help some of the poorer sections of society to help themselves.

Section summary
In this section you should have learned:
- What the Liberal Reforms did to help the old, young, sick and unemployed.
- How effective the Liberal Reforms were in dealing with the social problems facing Britain in the early 20th century.

Practise your skills

This section shows you how to plan an essay based on the question:

Between 1906 and 1914 the real causes of poverty were tackled successfully by government action. To what extent can this opinion be supported?

Remember – topic and task!
Decide what the question is about (the **topic**): the Liberal Reforms of 1906–14.
Decide what you have to do (the **task**): identify what you think were the main causes of poverty; judge how effective the reforms were in dealing with the main causes of poverty; decide whether or not you agree that the Liberal Reforms did sort out the problem of poverty.

Essay advice
The beginning
Your beginning must outline what you will do:
- You must show that you know what the causes of poverty were. Use the causes identified by Rowntree and Booth.
- You must then show that you know what the Liberal Reforms were.

The middle
Take each of the main causes of poverty – old age, sickness, unemployment and so on. Show in detail what the Liberals tried to do to help each problem.

The key words here are 'in detail'. This is an essay about the Liberal Reforms so you must show you know what they were.

You must also assess the reforms to decide how 'successfully' the Liberals dealt with the problems. You should combine knowledge of the causes of poverty and the Liberal Reforms with a consideration of their strengths and weaknesses.

Your conclusion

In your conclusion you should refer to the main question and show that you know there were strengths and weaknesses in the Liberal Reforms.

To help you write your conclusion look back to the examples at the end of previous chapters. In particular, look at the process model – in other words how to construct your conclusions.

Issue 6 – How successful was the Labour Government of 1945–51 in dealing with the social problems facing Britain after World War Two?

The big picture

In 1942 the Beveridge Report identified five key social problems that faced Britain. They were called the 'Five Giants'. In 1945 a new Labour government introduced a series of reforms that aimed to deal with each of the five giant problems identified by Beveridge. This issue looks at what Labour did and how successful they were at dealing with the 'Five Giants'.

World War Two had a big effect on the public's attitude towards the role of the government in their lives.

The phrase, 'Post-war must be better than pre-war' sums up public attitudes during the war. It meant that people wanted a better Britain after the war and even a Ministry of Health statement said that there could be 'no return to the pre-war position'.

Most historians accept that it was the effect of the war that prepared the way for a peace time welfare state. The government organised the rationing of food, clothing and fuel and gave extra milk and meals for expectant mothers and children. Evacuation of poor children from inner city areas to the suburbs alerted the middle classes of Britain to the real poverty that still existed in the industrial slums. Bombing of cities created vast areas that had to be rebuilt. Free hospital treatment for war-wounded – including bomb injuries for civilians, and free immunisation – are examples of the move towards a 'free' health service. To pay for these services the public got used to very high taxation levels.

By the end of the war both main political parties – Conservative and Labour – promised social reforms to improve health, housing and education.

The Beveridge report

An easy way to learn what Labour did is to know a bit about the Beveridge Report. The effect of the Beveridge Report was huge. Remember the report was published in 1942, three years before Labour came to power. Labour's reforms were based on the report so Labour could hardly claim to have created the ideas! Beveridge identified five main causes of hardship and poverty. He called them the 'Five Giants' blocking the path to progress. These giants were:

- want (poverty)
- disease (bad health)
- squalor (bad housing)
- ignorance (poor education)
- idleness (unemployment)

This cartoon appeared in 1942. Ten years later, would the soldier feel that Labour's social reforms justified his optimism?

The following diagram will help you to organise the main reforms and link them to Beveridge's five giants.

From the Cradle to the Grave

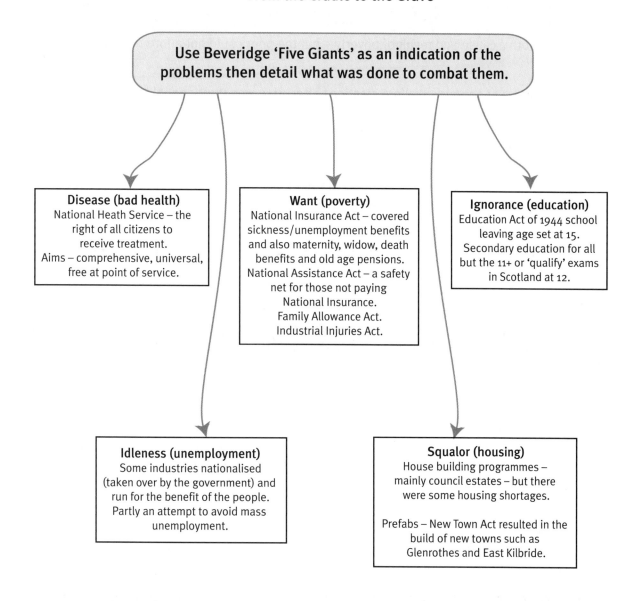

Use Beveridge 'Five Giants' as an indication of the problems then detail what was done to combat them.

Disease (bad health)
National Heath Service – the right of all citizens to receive treatment.
Aims – comprehensive, universal, free at point of service.

Want (poverty)
National Insurance Act – covered sickness/unemployment benefits and also maternity, widow, death benefits and old age pensions.
National Assistance Act – a safety net for those not paying National Insurance.
Family Allowance Act.
Industrial Injuries Act.

Ignorance (education)
Education Act of 1944 school leaving age set at 15.
Secondary education for all but the 11+ or 'qualify' exams in Scotland at 12.

Idleness (unemployment)
Some industries nationalised (taken over by the government) and run for the benefit of the people. Partly an attempt to avoid mass unemployment.

Squalor (housing)
House building programmes – mainly council estates – but there were some housing shortages.

Prefabs – New Town Act resulted in the build of new towns such as Glenrothes and East Kilbride.

The giant of want

The social problem that affected all others was poverty (called 'want' by Beveridge).

The solution?

The Family Allowance Act (started by the wartime government) paid a small amount of money to all mothers of two or more children.

The Industrial Injuries Act paid compensation for all injuries caused at work. It was paid by the government, not individual employers. All workers were covered.

The National Insurance Act of 1946 improved the old Liberal Act and allowed for sickness and unemployment benefits, retirement, widow's pensions and maternity grants. All people in work were included in this insurance. But what about those not in work?

The National Assistance Act helped people who were not in work or the old who had not paid enough contributions into the new National Insurance scheme. It was a safety net to ensure that nobody had to fall into poverty.

Was the solution successful?

By including all workers and families in the benefits scheme, it seemed this attack on poverty caused by shortage of money would be very helpful.

The giant of disease

Ill health was both a cause and result of poverty – but the poor could not afford medical treatment.

The solution?

The most important of Labour's Welfare creations after 1945 was the National Health Service (NHS). The NHS was based on three main aims:

- *Universal access*: the NHS was for everybody. The old health system, based on insurance schemes did not cover everyone.
- *Comprehensive*: the NHS would treat all medical problems.
- *Free at point of use*: no patient would be asked to pay for any treatment. In reality the service was, and is, paid for by the National Insurance payments made by every worker.

Was the solution successful?

The government inherited many out-of-date hospitals, costs were high and to keep doctors happy the NHS operated alongside private medicine. By 1950 the idea of 'free for all' treatment was damaged when charges were introduced for spectacles and dental treatment, but overall the NHS was welcomed and did provide medical help from 'the cradle to the grave'.

The giant of squalor

'Squalor' means bad housing and overcrowding. Most of Britain's cities still had slum areas, and overcrowding was still a serious problem made worse by bomb damage during the war.

The solution?

A fast house-building programme. The government aimed to build 200 000 houses each year. Most were council houses for rent. Many were factory-made houses, called 'pre-fabs' for short, which were quickly assembled on site. The New Towns Act in 1946 laid the plans for 14 New Towns to be built, including Glenrothes and East Kilbride. These were to be 'people-friendly' towns to relieve the housing problems in older cities.

Was the solution successful?

Many houses were built but Labour did not build as many houses as it promised. By 1951 there was still overcrowding and long waiting lists for council housing.

Some new industries moved to the New Town areas but often the towns became places where workers lived but they still commuted into the older towns for work.

The giant of ignorance

Many children received no education past primary stage and poorer parents could not afford the fees that some secondary schools charged.

The solution?

Labour put the Education Act of 1944 into operation, although the Act was the work of the wartime coalition government. The Education Act of 1944 raised the school leaving age to 15. All children were to get free secondary education. An exam at 11 (called the 11+ exam, or the 'qualy' in Scotland, which was short for the qualification exam) placed children in certain types of school. Those who passed the exam went to senior secondary schools, they were expected to stay on at school after 15 and go to university. Children who failed the exam went to junior secondary and were not expected to stay at school after 15. These children were expected to get unskilled jobs.

Was the solution successful?

For those who passed the 11+ exam or 'qualy' the system worked well. However those children who failed the exam seemed to be stuck in a trap of low expectations and inferior education. Many people opposed the idea of deciding a child's future at 11 or 12 years old.

The giant of idleness

In 1944 the government agreed to aim for 'full employment'.

The solution?

After the war there seemed to be work for everyone as Britain rebuilt itself. But Labour also nationalised certain industries, which means that the government took over the running of them. Be careful in discussing nationalisation in your exam. Some markers might think it is irrelevant because it was not a social reform, so it's up to you to make it relevant. Nationalisation was one way of keeping full employment as the government could use tax money to keep an industry going even if it was facing economic difficulties.

Was the solution successful?

Nationalisation was costly and at times led to bad management but in this part of the course it is not relevant to go into the economic arguments about nationalisation.

Section summary

In this section you should have learned:
- why the Beveridge Report is so important
- what is meant by a Welfare State
- what the Labour Government's social reforms were between 1945 and 1951
- the different points of view about Labour's part in the creation of the Welfare State
- how effective were the Labour Government's social reforms 1945–51 in dealing with problems facing Britain.

Practise your skills

This section shows you how to plan an essay based on the question:

How effective were Labour's reforms in dealing with the social problems facing Britain after World War Two?

Remember – topic and task!

Decide what the question is about (the topic): Labour's welfare reforms 1945–51.
Decide what you have to do (the task):
- Identify what the social problems facing Britain were in 1945.
- Decide whether or not Labour's reforms were effective in helping to solve the problems.

Essay advice

The beginning

Your beginning must outline what you will do. You should show you know what the social problems were – Beveridge did that work for you, so discuss his 'Five Giants'. Example:

Between 1945 and 1951 the Labour Government passed many social reforms aimed at defeating the giant problems identified by Beveridge in his report. Historians have argued for some time over how effectively each of the 'Five Giants' was tackled. Labour tackled each of the five giants with varying levels of success.

The middle

Take each of the 'Five Giants' and show in detail what the Labour government did to deal with the problem. The key words here are 'in detail'. This is an essay about Labour's reforms so don't waste time arguing whether or not Labour created a Welfare State. That is not part of this question.

You must also assess the reforms to decide how 'effectively' Labour dealt with the social problems:

- Did the reform solve the problem?
- Was the problem eased or made worse by the reforms?
- Was any failure of the reforms the fault of the Labour Government?
- Clearly poverty, ill health and bad housing still existed after 1951, so can Labour's reforms be described as a failure?

Your conclusion

By now you should know the process of writing an effective conclusion. If in doubt, refer to the examples at the end of previous chapters. Although the content in these other conclusions will not be relevant, the process and structure always is. Use the earlier models to construct an effective four-phase conclusion to this question.

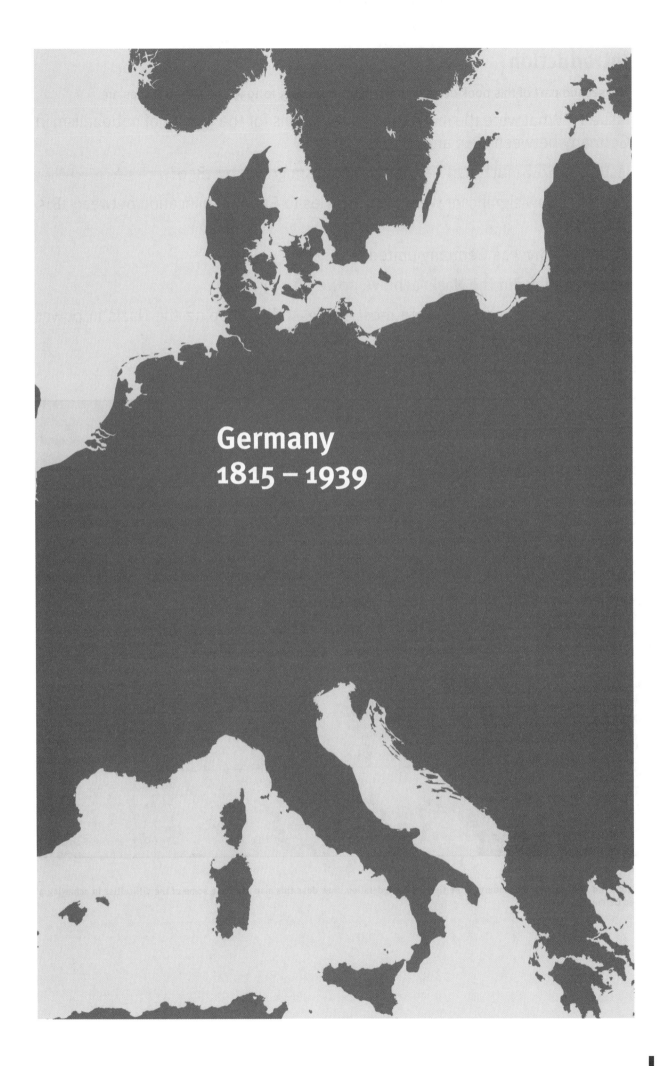

Germany
1815 – 1939

Introduction

The second part of this book deals with Germany from 1815 to 1939 and the six issues are:

Issue 1 – What were the most important reasons for the growth of nationalism in Germany between 1815 and 1850?

Issue 2 – How much had German nationalism grown by 1850?

Issue 3 – How significant were the obstacles to German unification between 1815 and 1871?

Issue 4 – Why was Germany united by 1871?

Issue 5 – Why did the Nazis achieve power in 1933?

Issue 6 – What methods were most successful in keeping the Nazis in power between 1933–1939?

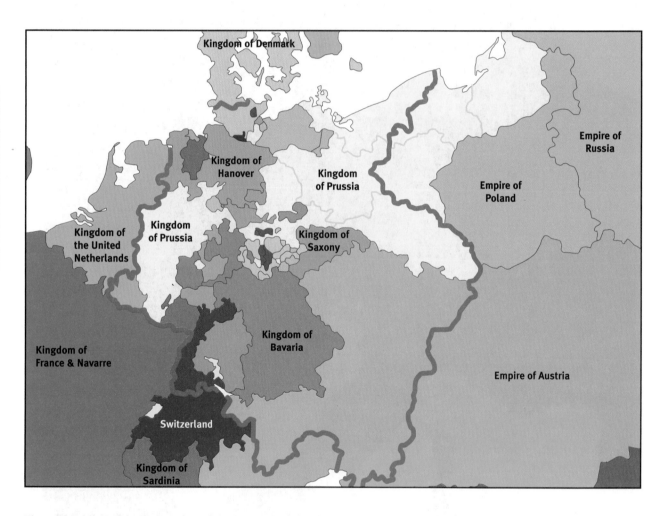

The solid red line marks the boundary of the German Confederation. How does this map illustrate some of the difficulties in achieving a united Germany?

Issue 1 – What were the most important reasons for the growth of nationalism in Germany between 1815 and 1850?

The big picture

The reasons for the growth of nationalism in Germany between 1815 and 1850 can be summed up in three phrases:

- political nationalism
- cultural nationalism
- economic nationalism

Political Nationalism grew with the spread of new ideas about Liberalism and Nationalism.

Nationalism was the desire of people with a common national identity to have their own country.

Liberalism was the desire to have a parliament where rulers were elected by the people of the country.

'Cultural nationalism' refers to the growth in feelings of a common identity linking the German states based on their common language, history and literature.

'Economic nationalism' is about the ways many German states became economically interlinked by 1850. Not all of these three reasons were equally important but all should be considered as influences moving the German states towards unification. To answer a question on this issue you must be able to reach a decision about how important each of these reasons was in moving Germany towards greater unity.

Political nationalism

Background

Before 1800 the country now called Germany was split into more than 400 separate states. Between 1800 and 1815 the German states had been conquered by the French leader Napoleon Bonaparte. Napoleon merged the hundreds of German states into 38 larger states, called the Confederation of the Rhine.

When Napoleon was defeated in 1815 the Confederation of the Rhine was replaced by the German Confederation. In 1815 Austria was the strongest European mainland power but new ideas like liberalism and nationalism threatened the unity of the Austrian Empire.

The man most associated with protecting the unity and power of the Austrian Empire was Prince Metternich. Metternich hoped to use the German Confederation to block any political change that would threaten the power of the old rulers.

Metternich also hoped to stop the spread of new ideas that might threaten his power, especially nationalism and liberalism. Metternich feared the spread of these new ideas and called them 'dark forces'.

Why did Metternich fear the spread of 'dark forces'?

If nationalism took root in the Austrian Empire the states within the Empire would want to break away to form their own nations. If liberalism took root in the Empire then Metternich's power and the power of the old powerful leaders would be weakened by parliaments representing the wishes of the ordinary people.

Was the German Confederation a move towards national unity?

Although it would be convenient to see the confederation as a step towards unification it would not be a fair assessment. In hindsight it looks as if the German Confederation fits into a pattern moving almost inevitably towards German unification. However in the early and mid 19th century that was not inevitable. The German states were divided and Austrian power too strong - and the rulers within the German Confederation did not support Liberalism or Nationalism.

This man is Prince Metternich. How did he personify so many of the obstacles to achieving German unification?

The German Confederation was mainly a renamed Confederation of the Rhine, with very few changes. The Assembly of the German Confederation - also called the DIET - represented the rulers of the German states, not the people. Rule 2 of the Confederation said 'the aim of the German Confederation is to ... guard the independence of the separate German states.'

The rise of Prussia

Prussia was a large German state in the north east of the German Confederation. Prussian forces were important in the final defeat of Napoleon at the battle of Waterloo in 1815. For that reason Prussia was rewarded with more land in the centre and west of Germany. The result was that Prussia became the biggest 'German' state and in hindsight it is possible to see the beginning of the rivalry between Austria and Prussia, which would not be ended until Prussia defeated Austria in the war of 1866.

Student societies and the Carlsbad Decrees

Feelings of a common German identity had grown under the French occupation. With a common enemy to dislike, many German students were attracted by the idea of a stronger and more united Germany. As part of their university courses, these students moved between the German states and so their nationalist ideas spread. Naturally the students hated Metternich, seeing him as a symbol of the old power they wanted removed.

In 1817, the conflict between Metternich and the students reached a peak at a festival in Wartburg, Saxony when a life-sized model of Metternich was thrown onto a fire. Metternich was furious and worried. If nationalist and liberal ideas spread, Austria's power would be weakened. The result was the Carlsbad Decrees of 1819, which banned student societies and censored newspapers. The following year the power of the DIET was increased so that soldiers could be ordered to stop the spread of new ideas in any of the German States. After the Carlsbad Decrees it seemed as if moves towards political nationalism were dead.

The 1848 revolutions

You can find out about the revolutions in Issue 2 but you should be aware of them in this issue too. Issue 1 covers the period up to 1850 so be careful when reading an essay question. If the title goes up to 1850 then the revolutions should be mentioned.

Revolutions occurred in most European countries during 1848. In March of that year, demonstrations took place in Berlin and other German cities. The old rulers seemed to give in quickly to the demands of the Nationalists and Liberals, especially when they heard that Metternich had been forced to run from Vienna.

Nationalists became linked with Liberals as these groups both wanted change.

Nationalists wanted the creation of a united country ruled by an elected national parliament. Liberals wanted freedom of speech, freedom of the press and political rights.

Both Liberals and Nationalists supported the revolutions of 1848. Those revolutions suggest there was growing support for nationalism in Germany but the failure of the revolutions to bring about big changes by 1850 suggest that nationalists were not yet strong enough to challenge the power of Austria.

Section summary

In this section you should have learned:

- what is meant by nationalism and liberalism
- why the German Confederation could not be described as a move towards unity
- why Metternich opposed nationalism and liberalism
- why political nationalism appeared almost dead by 1820
- how the seeds of future conflict were sown between Prussia and Austria.

Cultural Nationalism

In 1806 the head of the University of Berlin, Fichte, summed up the meaning of cultural nationalism when he wrote in his *Address to the German Nation* that Germans should see themselves as German rather than belonging to any small part of Germany. He described 'Germany' as the fatherland where all people spoke the same language and sang the same songs. He ended by saying that freedom is the right to be German and sort out one's own problems without interference from foreigners.

When Napoleon invaded the German states many Germans at first welcomed the French. They hoped the French would bring greater freedom to the German people. Instead Napoleon and the French soon became seen as occupiers and invaders of Germany who should be resisted. Although the German states had their differences, they all disliked the French invaders. That is really the point made by historian David Thomson in his book *Europe since Napoleon*, when he wrote, 'the French ... spread Liberalism by intention but created Nationalism by inadvertence. ' He meant the French intended to spread new political ideas (such as Liberalism) but, by defeating and occupying many of the German states, the French became a common enemy. The German states became united in a common feeling of resentment against the French.

During the French occupation of the German states many people began to identify with things that made them feel more 'German'. A sort of patriotic pride swept across the land. German poets and authors, such as the Grimm brothers, and composers such as Beethoven, encouraged feelings of national pride in the German states. By 1815, people in the German states became more aware, and proud, of their common culture. At the same time many Germans began to think in a more nationalist way and became more interested in their common culture. This was called 'cultural nationalism'.

Be careful. Cultural nationalism is a reason for the growing sense of German identity but there is some doubt over how important an influence it was in uniting Germany. Very few Germans could read and even less could afford to go to musical concerts to hear the music of Beethoven. Of course many Germans identified with stories of Germany's past and folk music sung at local get-togethers encouraging nationalist feelings. Historian Golo Mann, questioned the importance of cultural nationalism when he wrote that most Germans 'seldom looked up from the plough'. In other words most Germans either did not know about big national issues or were more concerned with surviving day to day.

Nevertheless issues of national identity, especially when under threat from foreign influences, did help national identity feelings to grow. One such example was the Rhine crisis of 1840 that you can read about later in this book.

Germany 1815 – 1939

Section summary

The growing popularity of German musicians and writers gave people a sense of belonging: in other words, a national identity was growing. That feeling of belonging was called 'cultural nationalism.' Cultural nationalism is a factor in the growth of German nationalism but perhaps not the most important one.

Economic nationalism and the Zollverein

You know that political nationalism was virtually dead between 1820 and 1848, suppressed by the Carlsbad Decrees. You also know that cultural nationalism was important to some people but to most Germans it was not vital to their everyday lives. However economic nationalism had a much greater effect on the lives of most Germans and as a result was an important factor in encouraging nationalist feeling.

The following diagram illustrates the greater importance of economic factors to the story of German Nationalism before 1848.

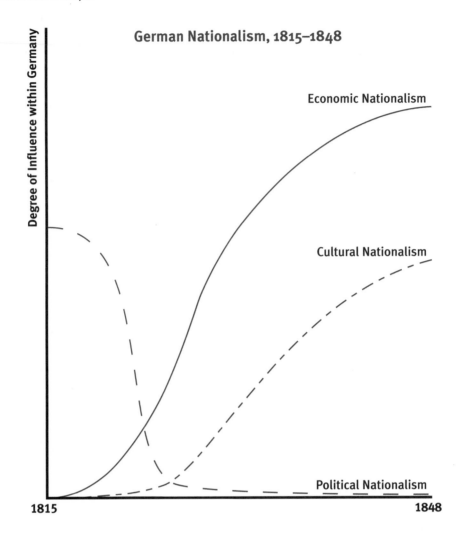

In 1815 Prussia was lucky in that it had coal and iron, the vital ingredients for an industrial revolution. As Prussia became richer other smaller states realised they could make money by trading more freely but trade between the states was difficult. To encourage trade, Prussia formed a customs union in 1818. That meant members of the union would not have to pay taxes on goods as they were transported from one member state to another.

By the 1830s the customs union was called the Zollverein. The Zollverein was very important because Prussia became a challenger to Austria for influence over the German states. The Zollverein was a prototype, or early example, of what would happen later – a 'united Germany' under Prussian control that excluded Austria.

The Zollverein didn't just help trade, it also helped nationalism to spread. As trade increased, ideas spread and different German states realised they benefited from closer contact with each other. The new railway network, centered in Prussia, also helped to bring German states together. Towns and cities grew in size. With more people living closer together new ideas spread more easily. By 1836 the Zollverein included 25 German states with a population of 26 million people.

Why was the Zollverein so important to later unification?
Simply, without the Zollverein, Prussia would not have had the muscle to defeat the power of Austria. The Zollverein brought German states together, excluded Austria and increased the power of Prussia.

Historian William Carr has called the Zollverein, 'The mighty lever of German unification.' Even in 1845 the Prussian foreign minister said 'Unification of states through trade will eventually lead to the creation of a unified political system under our leadership.'

Austria was excluded economically from the German states long before it was excluded politically.

Once Austria realised just how important the Zollverein had become it suggested a new organisation called the Zollunion under its own control but the plan was rejected by the other German states who thought their economic future lay with Prussia.

> ## Section summary
> In this section you should have learned what the Zollverein was, how it increased the power and influence of Prussia and how it can be seen as a prototype (or early version) of a Germany that excluded Austrian influence.

Practise your skills

This section shows you how to plan an essay based on this question:

Between 1815 and 1848 nothing of real significance happened to encourage the growth of German nationalism. How far can that view be supported?

Remember - topic and task !

Decide what the question is about (the topic) – it is about developments in German Nationalism between 1815-1848

Decide what you have to do (the task) – Use your knowledge to disagree with the view in the question and explain what did happen to encourage the growth of nationalism in Germany between 1815 and 1848. Your essay must have THREE main sections – an introduction, a series of paragraphs developing your introductory ideas and then finally a conclusion.

The beginning

Your introduction must outline what you will do. You have been given one opinion ('nothing of real significance happened') and you might choose to argue that was true about political Nationalism after the Carlsbad Decrees.

However you also know that things such as cultural Nationalism, the industrial revolution, the Zollverein and the spread of roads and railways all happened before 1848 so some things were happening. Mention all these points briefly in your introduction. All you are doing is showing the examiner you know what the question means and what direction your essay will take.

The middle

This is the place to show off what you know. Is there anything to support the point of view? Point out that with the banning of the student unions after the Carlsbad Decrees, not much political Nationalism happened. You could argue that politically Austria still dominated the Diet of the German Confederation and therefore German states but you could then say that other types of Nationalism were growing. That's a link to your next paragraph. Explain the importance of cultural Nationalism, give some examples of it, explain how it helped spread pride in Germany and how it helped moves towards unity. Move on to economic Nationalism. Explain how the industrial revolution changed Germany, how the Zollverein created changes that increased Prussia's power and how it helped make Germany more united.

It is often a good idea to let a marker know that you know about historical debate by using a quote giving the opposite point of view from the one in the title. What about using Carr's 'mighty lever' quote as a contrast?

Your conclusion

Finally you must have a conclusion. Your conclusion should answer the main question. It should sum up the points made and if possible suggest a debate between different ideas. In the case of this essay, use the evidence which might support the view that nothing happened, and contrast that with evidence that many things were moving Germany towards greater unity.

Here is an example:

Start by writing, '*In conclusion ...*' and write one sentence that makes a general answer to the main question such as '*In conclusion there were conflicting opinions about the growth of nationalism in*

Germany between 1815 and 1848.'

Then write, '*On one hand ...*' and summarise your information that supports one point of view about the essay title such as, '*On one hand it did seem that after the Carlsbad decrees that political nationalism made little progress.'*

Then write, '*On the other hand ...*' and here you must sum up the evidence that gives a different point of view about the main question such as, '*On the other hand, cultural nationalism encouraged the growth of a united German identity while economic nationalism showed the possibility of a united Germany under Prussian influence, which challenged the power of Austria.'*

Finally write, '*Overall ...*' and then write an overall answer to the main question, perhaps including what you think is the most important point made that led you to your final overall answer. For example, '*Overall, while it is true to say that German nationalism seemed to have made little progress on the surface by 1848, it is certainly not true that nothing happened. Prussian power had increased, German identity was strong and economic unity was setting the scene for greater political unity later.'*

Issue 2 – How much had German Nationalism grown by 1850?

> **The big picture**
>
> By 1850 it seemed that German unity was as far away as ever. Prussian ambitions had been crushed. Austria was back in control of the German Confederation. The Revolutions of 1848 had failed. You should know why they failed and what lessons the failure had for the future of Prussia and Germany.

What were the revolutions of 1848?

Across Europe the late 1840s had seen a series of bad harvests and potato famines. People were hungry and wanted changes to improve their lives. A rising middle class wanted more political influence. Nationalists and Liberals wanted political change. A series of revolts broke out across Europe against the old rulers who resisted any change. A revolution in France overthrew the king and then spread to the Austrian Empire, and Germany. None of the revolutions enjoyed any immediate success but the ideas sparked by the revolutions had far reaching consequences.

The 1848 revolution in Prussia

In March 1848 giant demonstrations rocked Berlin, capital of Prussia and at first the King, Frederick William IV, tried to stop the demonstrations by force. Eventually he decided to grant the demonstrators what they wanted. The King agreed that a new German parliament called a National Assembly would meet in the city of Frankfurt in May, 1848. He also declared, 'Today I take over the leadership of Germany. Today Prussia becomes the leader of a united Germany.' It looked as if support for nationalism was growing and would be further encouraged by the support of the King.

The 1848 revolutions – success or failure?

By the summer of 1848 it seemed as if the revolutions had succeeded. In many German states the old rulers had fallen from power. The German Confederation had crumbled. In Austria, Metternich had gone and Austria was distracted by revolutions within its own empire.

By 1850 it all seemed so different. The National Parliament in Frankfurt had collapsed. Germany was not united. King Frederick William IV had refused to lead a united Germany and Austria was back in control.

What went wrong?

There were three main reasons why the revolutions of 1848 failed.

The first reason involved suspicions between the poorer working classes and the more wealthy middle classes. The middle classes were happy enough to get rid of the Old Order but not when rioters attacked their property. The personal interest of the middle classes in their own property made them suspicious of the working classes who claimed to support nationalism but perhaps just wanted to grab as much for themselves as they could.

On the other hand, the working classes wanted a revolution to improve their living and working conditions. They didn't think those changes were likely in a parliament controlled by the middle classes who were also their employers. The different social classes could not unite when old authority reasserted its power. Self interest was more important than abstract ideas like nationalism.

A second reason for failure to agree within the Frankfurt Assembly was argument over the future shape of Germany. Should a united Germany be Grossdeutsch (including Austria) or Kleindeutsch (excluding Austria)?

States still friendly towards Austria and did not want Prussia to dominate the new Germany supported Grossdeutsch. Supporters of Kleindeutsch did not want to include Austria.

The third and vital reason for the failure of the 1848 revolution was the recovery of Austria and its allies in the German states. By 1849 the Austrian army was ready to crush opposition, bring back the old rulers and restore the Austrian controlled German Confederation. In contrast, the Frankfurt parliament was not strong enough, either politically or militarily, to resist Austria.

The fourth and final reason for the failure of the revolution was the lack of strong leadership. In the spring of 1848, King Frederick William IV of Prussia said he would lead a united Germany. However in March 1849 he refused the Crown of Germany. He said, 'I will not accept a crown from the gutter. It is a crown of shame.' The Frankfurt parliament was seriously weakened. Is the changing attitude of Frederick William really surprising? If Frederick William had tried to resist Austria he would have risked losing power again. In other words, King Frederick William IV was looking out for himself.

The Failure of the revolution – Erfurt and Olmutz
By the end of 1849 the Frankfurt parliament had crumbled, the revolution was left without a leader and the hopes of Liberals and Nationalists seemed to be dying.

However King Frederick William was still ambitious. He liked the idea of leading a united Germany, as long as a parliament did not control his actions, so in 1849 King Frederick William tried to create a different form of united assembly under his authority.

The Erfurt Union
The Erfurt Union was an assembly of German princes under Prussia's control. The German princes had little choice but to join, as powerful Prussia had ordered them to. However by 1850 it was obvious Frederick William had miscalculated. The German princes who felt they had been 'bullied' into the Erfurt Union now supported Austria as a balance against the Prussian king's ambition.

Austrian recovery
Austria was determined to destroy the Prussian challenge to its power. Schwarzenberg, the new Chancellor of Austria, said, 'Let Prussia be humiliated and destroyed. '

The struggle for influence between Prussia and Austria came to a head in 1850. A state called Hesse-Cassel, part of the Erfurt Union, asked for help to put down a small revolution. Austria and Prussia sent troops to help, both claiming their right to do so. For a time it looked as if war would break out between Prussia and Austria. The struggle grew into a showdown over who had power in the German states. At the last minute Prussia backed down and a meeting was arranged at Olmutz, which became known as 'The humiliation of Olmutz'.

At Olmutz:

- Prussia had to agree to the cancellation of the Erfurt Union.
- Prussia had to promise never again to challenge Austria's power.
- Before the Prussian and Austrian politicians met at Olmutz, it looked as if Prussia's chances of uniting Germany were ended.
- The old German Confederation was back in place.

Had the revolutions achieved anything?
Bismarck saw the failure of the revolution as a lesson for the future and he became convinced that only force could decide the future of Germany.

When talking about the future of Prussia and Germany, Bismarck said that the problems would not be solved; 'By speeches and majority votes – that was the mistake of 1848 and 1849. Germany does not look to Prussian Liberalism for its strength but to its power.'

Finally, it would also be wrong to see Olmutz as a crushing blow to Prussia. Prussia's political ambitions were put on hold but Prussia's real power, its economy and especially the Zollverein, was left untouched and it continued to grow rapidly in the 1850s. The revolutions of 1848 and 49 had turned the focus on political nationalism but economic nationalism continued behind the scenes.

Nationalism had grown considerably in the German states up to 1850 but there were still obstacles. One of those obstacles was the self-interest of various groups – the middle class, the working class or the king. They saw change in terms of what was best for their interests.

The growth of nationalism did not yet have enough support to challenge the practical power of those groups opposed to national growth – especially Austria.

Section summary

In this section you should have learned:
- why revolutions broke out in Germany in 1848
- why the revolutions failed
- why Austria seemed to be back in control of the German states by 1850
- what lessons were learned from the failure of the 1848 revolutions.

Practise your skills

This section shows you how to plan an essay based on the question:

To what extent had German nationalism only made limited progress up to 1848?

Remember - topic and task !

Decide what the question is about (the topic) – the amount of progress nationalism had made in Germany by 1848.

Decide what you have to do (the task) – explain how much progress Germany had made towards nationalism by 1848. Make clear that you understand what the question is asking you to do and outline the main ideas or arguments you will develop or explain in the middle section of the essay.

Here's a possible introduction to show you how it's done. Once again there are seven numbered points. Remember, it's a good tip to faintly number your main ideas – that tells you how many separate middle section paragraphs there should be based on the main points you 'signposted' in the introduction.

There were many reasons why German nationalism made so little progress by 1848, one of which was Austrian influence (1). Other factors that influenced the lack of progress with nationalism included opposition from the princes (2), divisions with Germany over religion and economy (3), the different hopes and aims of the middle and working classes (4) and also the argument over the future shape of Germany – Kleindeutsch or Grossdeutschland (5). A lack of leadership also restricted German nationalism (6). However on the other hand a lot more progress was made with economic and even cultural nationalism (7).

A good introduction will take time to think through, but without a good introduction your essay will go nowhere it will just tell a story. With this introduction you now have a structure and seven clear points to develop.

Your conclusion

Finally you must have a conclusion. As you may have read earlier your conclusion should sum up the points made and if possible suggest a debate between different ideas. In the case of this essay, refer to the amount of progress made towards nationalism by 1848. Was there only limited progress or had more been achieved?

Start by writing 'In conclusion.... and write one sentence that makes a general answer to the main question such as 'In conclusion German nationalism had made limited progress in some areas but greater progress in others'.

Then write 'One one hand..... and summarise your information that supports one point of view about the essay title such as 'Political nationalism had only made limited progress, especially after the Carlsbad Decrees'.

Then write 'On the other hand ...' and here you must sum up the evidence that gives a different point of view about the main question such as , 'On the other hand greater moves had been made towards German nationalism with the Zollverein'.

Finally write 'Overall .... and then write an overall answer to the main question , perhaps including what you think is the most important point to make in answer to the main question.

Issue 3 – How significant were the obstacles to German unification between 1815 and 1871?

Why was unification not certain by the 1850s?

Given the spread of Nationalism and Liberalism in the 19th century, some historians argue that German unification was inevitable however very few people would have predicted that Germany would be united twenty years after Olmutz. Austria was still dominant in Europe and in many ways remained a significant power until 1918. In the early 1850s it would have been difficult to see the process of German unification as inevitable in the near future. There were still many obstacles to unification.

The attitude of the German princes

Each of the states that made up Germany were ruled by a royal family and those families were reluctant to lose their power and influence. Not only did they wish to retain their own power, they were also fearful of an expanding Prussia. They feared Prussianisation – absorption into the Prussian state – and the loss of their influence and identity in an enlarged 'Germany'. As a result, the German princes wanted to turn the clock back to a time when their power and authority was unchallenged and the pressures of Nationalism and especially Liberalism did not threaten their existence.

Before 1815 it had all seemed so different. While Napoleon and the French forces occupied the German states, all of the German princes had promised their subjects a genuine constitutional government. Once the French had gone only six states kept their promise. The rulers of Prussia and Austria treated their solemn promises as mere bits of paper to be ripped up when it suited them. In 1851, Eduard Burckhardt published a booklet entitled *Proclamations and Promises Made by German Princes from 1813–1849*. The booklet was a complete collection of the meaningless promises made by the German Princes. All were broken.

In the early 1820s, nationalists reminded Frederick William III of Prussia of promises he had made. His reply was 'the question of time when to redeem the promise must be left to the decision of his majesty'. In the state of Hanover, farmers who had been freed by the French from being virtual slaves were once again returned to serfdom by their old rulers.

After the Carlsbad decrees, the German princes felt safe. Even the German tricolour flag was confiscated and a new edition of Fichte's *Address to the German Nation*, which had set alight nationalist hopes in 1806, was confiscated.

Professor Robert Prutz summed up the restrictions on freedom imposed by the princes between 1815 and 1830:

> 'For fifteen years they (the German princes) had been building and cementing their power, holding congresses, forming alliances, spreading the net of police supervision over the whole of Europe, filling prisons and building gallows.'

In July 1830, the princes were concerned when another revolution broke out in France, overthrowing the king. The revolution in France inspired students and young intellectuals in Central Europe to call for changes in their countries. Many of the young German writers and students wanted to destroy the old system of ruling the German states but the German princes retaliated by declaring in 1835:

> '... all German governments hereby assume the obligation to take action against the authors, publishers, printers, and distributors of the writings of the literary school known as Young Germany or Young Literature, and, by full force of the law, to suppress them by a lawful ban.'

By the mid 1830s the princes seemed safe. The revolutions of 1830 and 31 were short lived. When the revolutions of 1848 swept over Germany once again the princes offered change and once again when the power of Austria reasserted itself the princes forgot their promises and returned to their old ways. Once again the old order reasserted itself. Change would not happen until either it was in the princes' best interests to support change – or it was forced upon them.

Religious differences

In the 16th and 17th centuries, religious wars had ripped through the German states. The argument was essentially between supporters of the Catholic church and supporters of the Protestantism. Protestantism had grown out of dislike of some parts of the Roman Catholic faith. As time passed the conflict between religious groups died down but by the 19th century the different German states identified with and supported either Protestant beliefs or Catholic beliefs. The German states were in effect divided on religious grounds.

Roman Catholicism was strongest in the southern and western German states, while Protestantism was firmly established in the north-eastern and central regions. Religion also marked a main difference between the two strongest powers. Prussia in the north-east was Protestant while Catholic Austria supported, and was supported by, the Catholic German states. As the 19th century progressed the Catholic states were increasingly worried about Prussia's increasing influence. On the other hand, Protestant states were equally protective of their religious identity and were wary of closer links with Catholic states.

By the mid 19th century, there was no inevitability about unification. Religious divisions between the German states meant they were unlikely to choose unity because it would mean losing their separate religious identity.

Economic differences

The industrial revolution and the resulting growth in trade led the German states to realise it was in their interests to share resources. Slowly the states moved towards economic unification. For example, the growth of the railway network in Germany led to easier access to different resources across the German confederation. This helped to stimulate economic growth and meant that economic prosperity was increasingly reliant upon strong links between different member states of the German confederation. This led to the introduction of the Zollverein customs union. However, although the Zollverein helped increase prosperity and trade within member states, other states felt the Zollverein was mainly designed to increase the power of Prussia.

Southern states did not benefit from the economic growth of northern Germany. States more closely linked to Austria were mainly agricultural and much poorer. Those southern states looked to Austria for leadership but Austria was geographically limited. The main river in Austria is the Danube but that river flows into the Black Sea, the furthest point in Europe away from the growth areas of north-eastern Europe. Prussia's access to the river Rhine gave it a huge advantage.

The exclusion of Austria from the Zollverein was also a concern to many states. Although Prussia had invited Austria to join the Zollverein it was obvious to all that if Austria was to join it would be putting itself at a disadvantage. Prussia would be the leading power.

The differences between Prussia and Austria were further illustrated when Austria proposed its own customs union but given Austria's geographical position and limited natural resources it was never really an option.

Even states within the Zollverein benefiting from Prussian economic growth remained suspicious of Prussian ambitions. There was still no economic unity in Germany and suspicions between the northern, more industrial trading areas, and the southern, more agricultural areas, were yet more obstacles to unification.

The attitude of European powers

The German states were surrounded by three states all of whom opposed to unification. These states were Austria, France and Russia. None of those powers would welcome a strong united Germany pushing for influence in a new Europe.

Russia

Russia was a huge empire ruling many different nationalities. Not only was the Tsar friendly with the Austrian emperor, he was suspicious of any encouragement Prussia might give to Liberalism and Nationalism within the Russian empire. If those ideas took root in national areas within the Russian Empire, Russia would be faced with possible revolution. This was especially true in Poland, at that time under Russian control. The Poles were no strong allies of Russia and if nationalism grew in Poland then Russia would have difficulties. It was in Russia's interests to stop new ideas spreading. The last thing Russia wanted was an example of a new united nationalist Germany on its border.

France

France saw a united Germany as a threat to its own ambitions to expand its influence, perhaps towards the Rhineland. France's ambitions were most clearly seen in 1840 when France's parliament openly discussed the extension of its frontier to the Rhine. This would mean the taking over of the Prussian controlled Rhineland. The Germans were aware of their military weakness. Both Austria and Prussia at that time were not major military powers. The French threat was taken so seriously that writers appealed to the Germans to prepare themselves for armed resistance. In 1840 a poem called the *Watch on the Rhine* became hugely popular. It called for rivalries between the various German states to be set aside and for Germans to establish a unified state:

'The Rhine, the Rhine, go to our Rhine,
Who'll guard our River, hold the line?'

The French decided not to attempt to extend their border but their threat had encouraged a nationalism in Germany that the French both feared and disliked. A united Germany would challenge France for authority in Europe and France did not want that.

Britain

Britain was not entirely supportive of German unification. In the 1850s, Prussia and some smaller independent states in Germany were rapidly industrialising and growing in population. Railways criss-crossed Germany, and Germany was the centre of rail traffic on the European continent, taking trade away from British merchant ships. Economic predictions suggested by 1900 that a united Germany would be in the top three industrial producers in the world, behind the USA but challenging Britain for second position. It would also be twice as powerful as France. Britain and France had their own reasons for not supporting a united Germany.

Austria

Austria, as you know, was totally opposed to the rise of Prussia and moves to unification. As Chancellor Schwarzenberg said, 'We shall not let ourselves be thrown out of Germany.' Austria enjoyed its influential position in mainland Europe, and by controlling the German Confederation it could be said that Austria had influence from northern Europe to the Balkans.

But Austria was struggling. In the late 1850s Austria was involved in a war with France. Austria's army had suffered from inferior leadership, from lack of preparation and training and from insufficient transport. At the battle of Solferino in 1859, France and its Italian state allies from Piedmont-Sardinia defeated the Austrians. Fourteen thousand Austrians were killed and wounded. In July 1859, a compromise peace was established at the Conference of Villafranca. France gained land from Austria and the Austrians saw its possessions in the Italian states slipping from its grasp.

Austria did not only suffer military defeat. Austria had been isolated diplomatically during its war against France and wanted to revive its partnership with Prussia's monarchy against liberalism and nationalism.

The last thing that Austria wanted was any move towards German unity and a consequent decline in its own power and influence.

For all the reasons outlined above it should now be clear that German unification was an idea that had few significant supporters. It should be more of a surprise that Germany was unified only 20 years after Olmutz rather than seeing it all as a steady and inevitable progression to unity. There were many obstacles to unification.

Practise your skills

This section shows you how to plan an essay based on the question:

To what extent were economic and religious differences within the German states the main obstacles to unification during the 1850s?

Remember – topic and task!

Decide what the question is about (the topic) – what were the obstacles to German unification after 1850?

Decide what you have to do (the task) – show that you know that economic and religious differences were obstacles to unification but there were also other problems in the way of unification.

Essay advice

Introduction

Your introduction must make clear that you understand what the question is asking you to do and it must outline the main ideas or arguments you will develop or explain in the middle section of the essay. Here's a possible introduction to show you how it's done:

> There were many obstacles to unification during the 1850s – economic (1) and religious differences (2) were only two of them. The attitude of the German princes (3), the power of Austria (4) and the attitude of neighbouring powers (5) were three other obstacles and the lack of strong nationalist leadership (6) meant that those obstacles went mainly unchallenged in the 1850s.

The middle

Each of the numbered points should be developed with separate paragraphs showing your detailed and relevant knowledge.

Each paragraph should also make clear the link between your information and the overall question. In other words why the information included should be made clear. This is called your analysis where you USE your information to support your argument.

For example, here is a model paragraph from the middle part of an essay, developing the introduction point that economic differences were an obstacle to unification. Remember this is a development paragraph so you must show off detailed information and link to the question:

> Economic differences were only partly an obstacle to unification. Southern states were more closely linked to Austria and were mainly agricultural and much poorer. Those southern states looked to Austria rather than Prussia's Zollverein. The exclusion of Austria from the Zollverein also worried the southern states. They feared a Prussian take-over. Unfortunately Austria's own customs union failed to take root and the southern states felt even more isolated but fearful of where a united Germany under Prussia would lead them.
>
> On the other hand, it is not really true to say that economic differences were an obstacle to unification. The growth of the railway network in Germany led to easier access to different resources across the German Confederation. This helped to stimulate economic growth and meant that economic prosperity was increasingly reliant upon strong links between different member states of the German confederation. This led to the introduction of the Zollverein customs union. The influence of the Zollverein was an important factor for unification and perhaps the economic differences between the states were more based on political differences between the southern states and Prussia rather than major economic differences.

Your conclusion

Finally you must have a conclusion. As you may have read earlier, your conclusion should answer the main question. It should sum up the points made and if possible suggest a debate between different ideas. In the case of this essay try to weigh up the importance of different obstacles to unification. Some were more serious than others.

Start by writing, *'In conclusion ...'* and write one sentence that makes a general answer to the main question such as 'In conclusion there were many obstacles to unification.'

Then write, *'On one hand ...'* and summarise your information that supports the view that economic and religious differences were the most serious obstacles.

Then write, *'On the other hand ...'* and here you must sum up the evidence that gives a different point of view about other obstacles.

Finally write, *'Overall ...'* and then write an answer to the main question, perhaps including what you think is the most important obstacle to unification.

Issue 4 – Why was Germany united by 1871?

The big picture

By 1850, Prussian power seemed to have been destroyed, yet by 1860 Prussia had recovered and Austria had lost some of its influence. By 1871, Prussia had succeeded in uniting the German states under Prussian authority and Austria was severely weakened. The central person in all these events is Prussian Chancellor Otto von Bismarck. For many people, Bismarck was the reason why unification was achieved by 1871. How far can that opinion be supported?

Part 1: The 1850s and early Prussian recovery

A sign of Prussian recovery came in 1859 when a group of nationalist lawyers, teachers and businessmen formed a group that campaigned for national unification. It was called the Nationalverein. They said that the German Confederation should be replaced and it was the duty of every German to support Prussia in order to achieve firm, strong government.

Clearly, hopes for unification under Prussian leadership were still alive in 1859, nine years after the Olmutz 'humiliation'. The hopes of Nationalists were not dead.

Austrian power was weakening in the 1850s for several reasons

Economic weakness

Austria knew it would have to break up the Zollverein if Prussian economic strength was to be weakened. In 1852, Austria suggested making a new customs union to challenge the Zollverein but Austria had very few resources and had not yet experienced an industrial revolution. Nor did Austria have an easy communication network. Austria's main economic artery, the river Danube, flowed to the Black Sea and away from the industrial power houses of north western Europe. Austria was simply not in a position to offer other states strong reasons to join Austria's economic plan. The other states did not see how they would gain from it. The Austrian plan collapsed.

International isolation

For many years Austria had been allies with Russia but in 1854 the Crimean War broke out, with Russia fighting against Britain and France. When Russia asked for help, its old friend Austria refused. Russia was furious. Austria had lost an ally. In mainland Europe, only France remained as a powerful state, but in the 1850s Austria and France went to war against each other.

Military weakness

The image of the powerful Austrian army was weakened by a war fought against France and the Italian states in 1859. It showed that the Austrian army was not as powerful as it once had been. Reporters at the time described the, 'weak and disorganised' Austrian army as 'lurching from disaster to disaster'. Austria was defeated and lost land from its empire in Northern Italy. The Austrian army was exposed as weak, poorly equipped and out of touch with modern military tactics.

What were the consequences of a weakened Austria for German unification?

The 1850s saw one of the main obstacles to unification – Austrian power – being reduced in size. In contrast, Prussia was gaining strength, and evidence such as the Nationalverein shows that Prussia was seen as a possible 'leader' of a future united Germany. However, by 1860 it was still unlikely that German unification would take place simply because nationalists or liberals wanted it. Austria would naturally resist unification because it threatened its power. Only Prussia had the power to challenge Austria, but did Prussia want a united Germany?

Part 2: Bismarck arrives on the scene.

The big picture
In 1862 the Prussian King William I appointed Otto von Bismarck as Prussian minister, president and foreign minister. Bismarck became the vital figure in the unification of Germany but he was not a Nationalist. Nor was he a Liberal. Bismarck was a Prussian and supported authoritarian government. As he wrote in his autobiography, 'I would rather die with the King than give in to parliamentary government.'

Much of what Bismarck did was to increase the power and influence of Prussia and its King. If unification was the result then so be it!

An example of Bismarck's ruthless pragmatism is shown in his first dealings with the Prussian Landtag, which was the elected parliament of Prussia. Pragmatism means doing whatever is necessary to achieve the result you want. Simply put, the end justifies the means.

In 1857, Prussia's new king, William, wanted to increase the size of the army but the Landtag had to agree an increase in taxes to pay for the army reforms. They refused and the King was furious, believing that the Landtag should not have the right to block royal wishes. Bismarck advised the King to ignore the Landtag and simply order the Prussian people to pay the taxes. The Landtag was angry but the army reforms went ahead. The King was very grateful to Bismarck, who became Minister-President of Prussia.

This is Otto von Bismarck. Some say he was the architect of German unification. What do you think?

Bismarck knew an efficient, powerful army might be necessary in the near future. After the failure of the 1848 revolution, he wrote, 'Germany does not look to Prussian Liberalism, but to its power ... Not by speeches and majority verdicts will the great decisions of the time be made ... but by iron and blood.'

After the dispute with the Landtag was resolved, Bismarck now had the opportunity and resources to order the development of Prussia's army.

Section summary
In this section you should have learned:
- that in the 1850s Austrian power was declining
- that Bismarck became Minister-President of Prussia
- that Bismarck was determined to support the power of the Prussian king and build up the power of the Prussian army.

Part 3: The wars of unification

At a glance
Prussia was victorious in three wars – against Denmark in 1864, Austria in 1866 and France between 1870 and 1871. The result of the wars was an increase in the power of Prussia and the unification of Germany, and ever since historians have argued over how important Bismarck was to the process of unification.

The war with Denmark

Bismarck's first step in weakening Austria's power was a war with Denmark.

In 1863, a new Danish king came to the throne who wanted more power over the two areas on the Danish/German Confederation border called Schleswig and Holstein. It is unlikely you will need to know the details of the row that erupted over Schleswig and Holstein. What is more important is how Bismarck used the row to his advantage.

When the Danish king took over Schleswig, Bismarck suggested that a combined Prussian and Austrian force should attack Denmark. Denmark was quickly defeated and Prussia gained the glory as defender of German interests. The Treaty of Vienna ended the war between Denmark and Prussia.

Denmark gave up its claims to Schleswig and Holstein but no agreement was reached about what was to happen to the Duchies until 1865 when, at the Convention of Gastein (August 1865), it was agreed that Holstein would be run by Austria and Schleswig would be run by Prussia.

What did Bismarck gain from the conflict with Denmark?

Prussia's status within the German Confederation was boosted, as it looked as if Prussia was a supporter of Nationalism against the threat of Denmark. The recently reformed Prussian army was tested in an 'easy' war before any conflict with Austria erupted.

Bismarck knew that if Prussia was to be the most powerful state in Germany, Austrian power would have to be weakened – but not yet. Austria could not refuse to get involved in the row with Denmark if it wanted to keep its influence over the German Confederation. At the Convention of Gastein, Austria was politically and militarily cornered by Bismarck. A war with Austria could be provoked when it suited Bismarck.

The second war of unification, Prussia v. Austria (1866)

Some historians support the view that Bismarck was an opportunist who used coincidental events to his advantage. However in this case it is clear that Bismarck deliberately planned the conflict with Austria.

How did Bismarck put his plans into action?

It is vital in any consideration of Bismarck's importance to unification to understand what he did to prepare the way for military victory.

First of all, Bismarck had to deal with the possibility that in any war with Austria, the other European powers might decide to support Austria or try to grab influence for themselves. The two main powers Bismarck had to 'neutralise' were Russia and France.

Making friends with Russia

Recent historians have argued that the promise to support Russia was not part of Bismarck's deliberate plan to isolate Austria, but you can still use it as part of your argument.

Bismarck wanted to ensure that when Prussia fought Austria, Russia would not get involved.

In 1863, a nationalist revolt broke out in present-day Poland, which was then a part of Russia. The aim of the Poles was to break away from Russia and create their own country, and most of Europe was sympathetic to the Poles. However, when Russian forces attacked the Poles, Bismarck gained Russian friendship by stopping Polish refugees escaping across their border into Prussia.

By 1865, Bismarck was fairly certain Russia, formerly a friend of Austria, was now less likely to take sides against Prussia in any future row with Austria.

Keeping France neutral

Bismarck knew there was a possibility that France might help Austria as both were Catholic countries and suspicious of Prussia. Bismarck had to make sure that France would not get involved in a war between Austria and Prussia.

In October 1865, Bismarck arranged a meeting with the French leader Napoleon III at a French seaside resort called Biarritz. Without making any promises, Bismarck hinted very strongly that France would get extra territory, possibly in the Rhineland, if France stayed out of a war between Prussia and Austria. Napoleon even believed secretly that a war between Prussia and Austria would benefit France by weakening France's two main competitors in Europe.

Doing a deal with Italy
Bismarck also knew that Austria was having trouble in Italy. At that time most of northern Italy was part of the Austrian Empire. Bismarck knew that if he could persuade Italian nationalists to attack Austria from the south at the same time as fighting Prussia to the north, Austria would have to split its armies.

Bismarck suggested a secret alliance between Prussia and Italy. Bismarck promised Italy the land around the city of Venice called Venetia if Italy helped Prussia fight a war against Austria. Italy agreed.

By 1866 Bismarck had set the diplomatic scene. He was ready to fight.

War with Austria
Bismarck used the unresolved situation left after the Convention of Gastein in Schleswig/Holstein to complain that Austria was not running Holstein properly. Bismarck complained that Austria was stirring up anti-Prussian feelings in Schleswig. Prussian troops marched into Holstein.

Austria asked the German Confederation for support and when some states (mostly Catholic south German states fearful of a powerful Prussia) agreed to resist Prussia, Bismarck had what he wanted – an excuse to attack, defeat and take over the smaller states in Germany that supported Austria.

Meanwhile, as part of the agreement between Italy and Prussia, Italy attacked Austria. Austria mobilised all its troops and Bismarck used that as an excuse to claim Austria was getting ready to attack Prussia. Prussia attacked Austria in July 1866.

On 3 July 1866, a battle was fought at Koniggratz (also called the 'Battle of Sadowa'). The Austrian army was defeated but suddenly Bismarck insisted on ending the war. It had never been his intention to destroy Austria, only Austria's influence over Germany. Bismarck did what was necessary to achieve his aim - and nothing more.

The Treaty of Prague
The Treaty of Prague ended the war between Prussia and Austria and is a good demonstration of **realpolitik**.

The German Confederation was ended and by the end of 1866 a North German Confederation had been created. Most of it was Prussian territory. There was also a much weaker South German Confederation.

Austria was treated quite well despite some Prussians, including the King, who wanted to crush Austria.

A Kleindeutsch had been created – a North German state without Austrian influence – and it seemed as if Germany was close to unity. Prussian Liberals were so pleased that most of Germany was united that they forgave Bismarck for the earlier row over army reforms. After all, Bismarck had given them unity by 'blood and iron'.

The third war of unification – France

Bismarck and the Franco-Prussian War
In 1866, the southern states of Germany were still outside the North German Confederation. They only became part of a united Germany after the third of Bismarck's wars, against France, in 1870.

The war with France is used by historians as an example of Bismarck seeing an opportunity arise from situations outwith his control, but that he used to his advantage. The facts certainly support such an opinion.

Bismarck could not simply declare war on France. He needed to set up a situation that would make France appear to be in the wrong. Bismarck's chance came when a row broke out over who was to be the next king of Spain!

The Hohenzollern Candidature
In 1868, a revolution in Spain led to a search for a new ruler. A distant relative of the Spanish royal family was found, called Leopold of Hohenzollern, but Leopold was a Prussian. France was worried because, in the event of a future conflict, France might be trapped between a strong Prussia to the north of France and a Prussian 'puppet' government in Spain to the south.

The French protested strongly and even insisted that the Hohenzollern family should give up their claim to the Spanish throne forever.

The Ems telegram

King William was on holiday at a health resort called Ems when he got the French demand. William politely refused the French demand and sent a telegram to Bismarck telling him what had happened and how he intended to reply to the French.

Bismarck saw his chance and altered the telegram slightly so that it appeared the King had insulted the French ambassador by refusing to meet him. Bismarck then sent his version of the Ems Telegram to the French and German newspapers for publication. The edited version of the telegram had the effect that Bismarck intended. The French public demanded war because of the 'Prussian insult'. France declared war. Bismarck had got what he wanted.

Germany united – at last!

Within a few weeks of France declaring war, the French army was crushed at the battle of Sedan and France surrendered in January 1871. The North German Confederation and the South German States (who had realised their only chance of security was as part of a united, strong Germany) united. In the Palace of Versailles just outside Paris the German princes proclaimed King William of Prussia as the new German Emperor or Kaiser.

Prussianisation or unification?

Was Germany united – or Prussianised? There is a view that the process of German unification should really be seen as the story of Prussia's growing power.

Historians still debate the word 'united', because it suggests states coming together through choice. However Bavaria was bribed by Bismarck to join the new Germany and many smaller states still believed they had been defeated and absorbed by Prussia rather than choosing to unify.

It is true that the Prussian King became the German Kaiser and that Bismarck became the German Chancellor. Prussian taxes and laws became German taxes and laws. Such evidence suggests that the German states had been 'Prussianised' rather than united, but the fact is that 'Germany' existed from 1871.

Section summary

In this section you should have learned:

- Prussia fought and won three wars between 1864 and 1871.
- The three wars were all very important in the story of unification.
- The wars were against Denmark, Austria and France.
- Bismarck used diplomacy and planning to make sure that Prussia won.
- Bismarck used 'lucky breaks' to Prussia's advantage.
- By 1871 Germany was united, but it was a Germany under the influence of a very strong Prussian state.

Part 4: How important was Bismarck to unification?

There are three main opinions:

- Bismarck's importance is that he operated like an architect who had a master plan that he followed in order to build a united Germany.
- Bismarck acted as a catalyst to speed up change that would have happened anyway. Changes such as the Zollverein, the spread of railways and growing Nationalism would have united Germany eventually.
- Bismarck had the political skill to take advantage of circumstances as they arose, and over which he often had no direct control. Supporters of this view believe Bismarck was an opportunist – taking advantage of situations as they arose.

Be careful if you are arguing that Bismarck had a master plan. Students often use, as evidence of Bismarck's plans, a conversation that Bismarck was supposed to have had with a British politician in which he outlined how he intended to unite Germany. There is no proof the conversation ever took place! An account of the alleged conversation only appeared nearly 20 years after the events took place.

It is also difficult to decide if Bismarck himself was always telling the truth – especially in his memoirs. In 1890, Bismarck wrote:

> 'I was like a man wandering in a forest. I knew roughly where I was going but I didn't know exactly where I would come out of the wood at.'

Was Bismarck just being modest?

So what is the correct answer to the question 'Did Bismarck have a master plan?' The safest answer, and the nearest to the truth, is that Bismarck used his talents to unite Germany, but he was very aware of circumstances, coincidences and pre-existent factors that helped him to achieve his aim. The fact is that Bismarck did fight three wars, which resulted in unification. Bismarck, in the words of one historian, was like a card player who, although he did not deal the cards, played his hand very well.

Section summary
In this section you should have learned:
- Historians still argue over the importance of Bismarck to the unification of Germany.
- Some say Bismarck was the main reason why Germany was united.
- Some argue that unification was the inevitable result of economic and political trends in Europe.
- Other historians say that unification was mainly the result of lucky opportunism.

Practise your skills

This section shows you how to plan an essay based on the question:

There was nothing inevitable about German Unification. Although Bismarck made the use of his chances, he would not have succeeded without good luck. How far can that view be supported?

Remember – topic and task!
Decide what the question is about (the topic) – this question is mainly about Bismarck's role in the process of German unification.

Decide what you have to do (the task) – the first part of the question refers to the argument that unification would have happened anyway, regardless of Bismarck, because of the pressures that were increasing in the 19th century.

The second part of the question asks about Bismarck's importance. You must decide how far Bismarck's skills were important, how far he was just lucky and also what other factors were pushing Germany towards unification.

Essay advice.
The beginning
Your beginning must outline what you will do. You could start by setting the context. Then indicate the three sections of this essay. Firstly, sketch the developments that laid the foundations of unification before the 1860s, such as Prussian economic power, the Zollverein and Austria's declining power. Secondly, outline the importance of Bismarck's diplomacy. Finally, raise the issue of circumstances that arose which Bismarck used to his advantage. In other words signpost the main directions your essay will take.

The middle
It's vital in the 'middle sections' of essays to showcase your detailed knowledge. Don't waffle – be precise and accurate.

Explain more fully why Prussia was seen as a focus for nationalist hopes before 1860. How realistic is the case that German unification was inevitable?

The bulk of your answer must be on Bismarck: his diplomacy and strategy, his three wars and how he 'Prussianised' the German states. But beware not to turn the essay into a story of the three wars. Within your section on Bismarck it is inevitable that you will deal with situations and events which cropped up outwith Bismarck's control, but which he used to his advantage. Consider their importance. Would Bismarck have been so successful without these events? Or does the importance of these events lay in the way Bismarck used them for his own ends? How far was Bismarck a catalyst? (Remember this counts as argument or analysis).

The questions raised in this section are vital to your overall answer. Look back at the title and you will see all of these questions are part of the overall answer.

Your conclusion

A conclusion should have four main stages:

- The first stage is the first sentence where you restate the core issue of the question.
- The second stage could start, 'On one hand ...' and introduce one side of your balanced conclusion.
- The third stage could start with, 'On the other hand' and present some evidence that balances or counters your earlier evidence.
- Your final stage is where you weigh up your two sides and make your overall decision, perhaps starting with 'On balance ...'

Example

In conclusion, the debate about Bismarck's importance to German unification continues. On one hand, without a reformed army, a revived economy, nationalist enthusiasm and several coincidental pieces of luck such as the Hohenzollern Candidature, Bismarck could not have united Germany. On the other hand, it is not enough to argue that Bismarck was just lucky in the sense of the 'right man in the right place at the right time'. Bismarck was a catalyst and although he did not always control events, he had the ability to use the opportunities they offered.

On balance, in 1861 Germany was as divided as ever. Ten years later Germany had been united or at least Prussianised. This was due to the work of Bismarck.

The Link

Your Higher History course covering Germany 1815–1939 now jumps from 1871, when Germany was united, up to 1918 when Germany was defeated in the First World War.

The following section is not part of your examination but provides a link between 1871 and 1918 when the course starts again. The purpose of this link is simply to let you see the big picture and how the story of Germany between 1815 and 1939 fits together. It might also help to explain why democracy failed in the 1920s and why by the early 1930s Germany fell under the influence of Hitler and the Nazis.

Between 1871 and 1914, Germany's relationship with the rest of Europe was controlled by two people: Bismarck until 1890 and then Kaiser Willhelm II. Bismarck wanted to protect the new nation of Germany. To do that he created a complex web of alliances with other countries. It was called 'The Bismarck system'. Others called it 'a balance of tensions'.

After Bismarck's resignation in 1890, the importance of the Chancellor within German politics declined as the authority of the new Kaiser, Willhelm II, increased.

In 1890 Germany was a modern industrial power but political reform had not accompanied economic developments. Kaiser Willhelm II called the Reichstag, elected by the people of Germany, 'an ape house'. The German Constitution had no restraining influence on the Kaiser who could appoint and dismiss ministers as he wished. The Kaiser himself was a supporter of traditional authority. He declared, 'I intend to rule as well as reign '. It seemed unlikely that the Kaiser would agree to demands for greater democracy.

When the Kaiser took over the direction of German foreign policy in 1890 he wanted to increase German influence in the world. Unfortunately he seemed not to understand the 'Bismarck System' of using alliances to maintain peace. Instead, the Kaiser's foreign policy scared other countries so that by 1914 he faced powerful enemies and Europe was divided into 'two armed camps'. In that year he allowed Germany to get dragged into a Balkan war, which Bismarck had always tried to avoid. The crisis in the Balkans that triggered the outbreak of the First World War, which had its roots in Bismarck's 'balance of tensions', was made worse by the Kaiser's actions.

Some historians argue that the Kaiser was prepared to use an aggressive foreign policy to distract attention from domestic problems. However it is important not to think of the Kaiser as unpopular in Germany. Until 1918, he was a respected, even loved, leader. It took the shock of defeat in the Great War to increase discontent with his autocratic rule and provoke a revolution. Even then, in the years that followed, many Germans longed for the good old days of the Kaiser when Germany was respected and there were no difficult political choices to make.

Issue 5 – Why did the Nazis achieve power in 1933?

The big picture

The new Germany that emerged at the end of the Great War had a new political system called a 'republic'. The republic was a democracy based on a written constitution guaranteeing individual freedoms. The new constitution was written in a town called Weimar, hence the name the Weimar Republic.

Unfortunately, Weimar Germany was identified with failure and defeat and the new political system was challenged by various groups who did not share the political beliefs of the new Germany. One of these groups was the Nazis, led by Adolf Hitler.

Hitler came to power promising a new Germany with strong leadership in contrast to the lack of authority within Weimar Germany.

The failure of the Weimar Republic

In this part of the course there are three main questions to prepare for.

- Why did the Weimar democracy fail?
- Why did Hitler come to power in Germany?
- How did Hitler come to power in Germany?

The chart below summarises the main ideas linked to the failure of the Weimar Republic. The rest of this unit looks closely at these ideas.

Germany 1815 – 1939

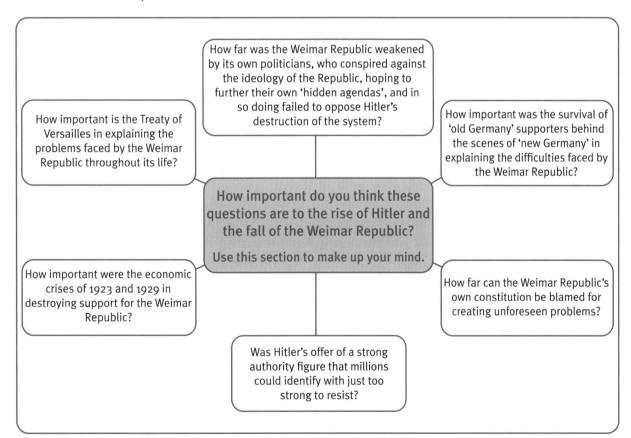

The new Weimar Republic was unpopular for four main reasons.

Reason 1: the new government was blamed for the Treaty of Versailles

On 28 June 1919, the victorious allies made Germany sign the Treaty of Versailles, which many Germans called a 'Diktat' – a dictated treaty that was forced on them. Germany was forced to accept blame for causing the war and also all the deaths and destruction that resulted from the war.

Germany lost all colonies, much of its industrial resources, some areas of land and its armed forces were severely cut.

Germany also had to pay compensation, called reparations, to the victorious powers.

Throughout the 1920s many nationalist groups claimed the new republic 'stabbed Germany in the back' by accepting the Treaty. Nationalists made it clear they identified the new government with defeat and humiliation, regardless of the truth or otherwise of that claim.

The 'stab in the back' idea is nonsense. Germany's armies had been broken and if Germany had not signed, the allies would have invaded Germany. However the German public found it easier to accept the 'stab in the back' myth than accept that Germany had been defeated.

The treaty is an important factor in understanding why Weimar Republic collapsed. Although they had no choice but to sign, the Weimar politicians were associated with the humiliation of the Versailles Treaty.

Reason 2: the new government had very few supporters

The Weimar Republic was weakened by several political groups that opposed democratic principles. You must be clear why Weimar was opposed by political groups on both the left and right wings.

Enemies on the left

In 1919 the Spartacists, who were revolutionary socialists and who later became known as the Communist Party or KPD, tried to start a revolution to create a new Communist Germany.

The Spartacist rising was defeated with great brutality by an alliance between the new socialist government, the regular army and gangs of ex-soldiers called 'Freikorps'. Ten years later, when Hitler was rising to power, the hatred felt by the Communists towards the SPD (Social Democratic Party) for destroying the Spartacist rising prevented the left wing from uniting against Hitler in elections.

Enemies on the right

New Germany was equally hated by the right wing. When the Weimar government tried to carry out the military cuts imposed by the Versailles treaty, German officers were furious. These officers saw an end to their careers and supported the Kapp Putsch – an attempt to overthrow the government and bring the Kaiser back.

However, don't think of the right wing as simply a collection of military leaders. The right included many professionals whose early careers had been spent within the Imperial Germany of the Kaiser. Although the government changed after the war and became a democracy, most of the professional classes did not necessarily change their attitudes. All these people still identified with 'old' Germany while working within new Germany. They were unlikely to support the new democracy when a crisis arose in the early 1930s.

Reason 3: weakness and confusion within the new democratic system made people discontented

The new democratic constitution of Germany was called 'the most perfect democracy on paper' but it had flaws that were exploited by opponents. Although the constitution was written to make a fair and democratic system, confusion about the voting system and the power of the President increased discontent.

The voting system was based on proportional representation. That means there was never any clear winner at elections. Deals had to be done between parties and coalition governments set up. These coalition governments were unlikely to put into action strong decisive policies. Between 1919 and 1930 there were 13 coalition governments.

Although the voting system was meant to be fair to all political parties it was confusing for voters. The system also allowed small, extremist parties such as the Nazis and the Communists to gain some representation in the Reichstag – even if these parties really aimed at the destruction of the new republic.

The President was the head of the new republic and he was meant to represent stability and continuity as he did not change when political parties struggled for power.

Creators of the constitution realised that future crises might occur and fast decisive action might be needed to protect the new democracy. Article 48 was created to allow for fast decision-making to deal with emergencies. Article 48 gave the President (elected every seven years) the power to rule in an emergency without needing approval from the Reichstag. But what might happen if an extreme politician – such as Hitler – gained control over the President?

Reason 4: Germans blamed the Weimar Republic for economic difficulties, especially the hyperinflation of 1923 and the 1929 Depression

The Treaty of Versailles ordered Germany to pay compensation to the victorious allies but by 1923 France was angry with Germany's repeated failure to pay the instalments on time. The result was that in 1923 France, with Belgian help, invaded the Ruhr, Germany's industrial heartland.

The French had hoped to force Germany to pay up. Instead, Germany went on strike. The German government printed more and more paper money to pay the strikers, but with no wealth being created the German currency collapsed and by November 1923 it was worthless. This was the time of hyperinflation. Almost overnight the life-savings of thousands of Germans became worthless and they blamed the government.

You cannot over-stress the impact hyperinflation had on the German people, especially the middle classes. It was described as 'the scar that never healed'.

The German economic crisis of the early 1920s only ended when American money was pumped into the German economy and a time of relative political and economic stability followed.

When the American economy collapsed in 1929 and US money was withdrawn from Germany, unemployment began to rise fast. Many Germans were worried that the nightmare of 1923 was about to return. They blamed the government.

Section summary
In this section you should have learned that:
- the new democratic Weimar Republic had many enemies but few friends
- the new democratic Weimar Republic had flaws in it which could be exploited by groups that wanted to destroy Weimar
- many Germans blamed the Weimar Government for all their problems.

The Weimar Republic was weakened by the rising appeal of the Nazis after 1929

In 1928 the Nazis had 12 seats in the Reichstag but by 1930 they had 108. You can use these figures to introduce an answer about the rise of the Nazis because clearly something must have happened between 1928 and 1930 to increase Nazi support. The answer lies in 1929 – in that year Germany was hit by a double disaster.

The first disaster was the death of Gustav Stresemann. He was the politician in the 1920s who had done most to give Weimar Germany stability and international respect. Under Stresemann, Germany was recovering and his death came to symbolise the end of the 'golden years' of Weimar Germany.

The second disaster was the Wall Street Crash. You don't need to know the economic details of the Crash but you do need to know the results. As American banks collapsed they demanded the return of the loans they had made to Germany. With the end of the US loans, Germany went into depression. Unemployment rocketed and Germany descended into economic chaos. Although hyperinflation did not return, the German public remembered the nightmare of 1923 and 'the scar that never healed'. By 1930 the German public was desperate for a saviour to help them out of the mess.

The economic crash was the catalyst that transformed the appeal of the Nazis. As the historian A.J.P. Taylor said, 'It was the Great Depression that put the wind in Hitler's sails'.

In 1930 the Nazis made their big breakthrough into mainstream German politics. The Nazis appeared to be strong and decisive. In 1923 the Nazis had tried to grab power in Munich but they failed, Hitler was arrested and sentenced to a short term in prison. The shortness of his prison sentence is in itself important. When the left wing tried to overthrow the government in 1919–20 they were murdered, arrested and executed or given long prison sentences. Three years later Hitler served less than a year in prison for the same crime. Hitler seemed to have friends in high places. That's an important point to make in any answer about the rise of Hitler.

Another point to make is the decision Hitler reached in prison about how the Nazis would rise to power. He is often reported as saying, 'we must hold our noses and enter the Reichstag'. In other words, Hitler would campaign for power legally and destroy from within the system he despised.

However, the Nazis were not the only party that despised the ideology and identity of Weimar Germany. By 1930, Nationalist groups led by Alfred Hugenberg saw the Nazis as a possible route to power. Hitler was happy to use Hugenberg, who owned most of Germany's new cinema industry and hundreds of local newspapers. Hitler saw a way of becoming a nationally known figure very quickly in a pre-television age.

All Hitler needed was the opportunity to spread his message of a new Germany under Nazism. Events in 1929 gave Hitler his opportunity.

Nazi ideology – what was Nazism?

Most political parties have a clear idea of what they stand for and also a clear plan that is designed to appeal to certain sections of the population.

The Nazis tried to be all things to all people. As one of many small political groups in the early 1920s the Nazis had to attract attention and support.

A definition of Nazism could include the following:

- One strong leader: Hitler has been described as the buckle holding the belt of Nazism together.
- Centralised government tried to control everything. Regional and local Nazi organisations were established so that control extended throughout the whole country.
- Only one political party: all opposition was banned.
- Propaganda was used to increase Nazi power and control the media.
- Racism: Hitler used feelings of nationalism, patriotism and racism to create a belief that Germans were the master race.
- Anti-Semitism: Hitler claimed that Germany had been stabbed in the back by Jewish politicians in 1918. He blamed Germany's economic problems on Jews. Hitler even claimed Communism was a Jewish plot because the founder of Communism, Karl Marx, was a Jew. By the early 1930s it suited many Germans to see the Jews as an excuse for Germany's difficulties.

Hitler provided simplistic answers to complex problems and the removal of difficult decisions. Nazi Germany was an authoritarian state, which insisted on obedience to the rules of the state. The following description sums up the aims of a totalitarian, authoritarian state: 'Nothing outside the State, everything within the State, nothing against the State.' Nazi Germany was a dictatorship, but one that attracted support from people looking for a saviour.

Section summary

In this section you should have learned:
- how the Nazis tried to be all things to all people to attract public support
- that Nazi ideology was authoritarian and racist
- that Nazi ideology was a mixture of old and new ideas.

In January 1933, Hitler was invited to be Chancellor of Germany. In this section you must deal with three main characters – President Hindenburg (don't get confused with Hugenburg, the owner of cinemas and newspapers), Von Papen and Von Schleicher who were vital for Hitler's rise to 'respectable' power.

President Hindenburg was an old war hero who represented old style authority and personified 'Old Germany'. But he was very old, almost senile and the authority of Hindenburg was used by politicians who wanted to undermine Weimar democracy.

President Hindenburg and other Weimar politicians had been acting in an undemocratic way since 1930. For example, Hindenburg, by using Article 48, allowed Chancellor Bruning to govern Germany for almost two years without majority support in the Reichstag.

As Hitler and the Nazis rose in popularity, Weimar politicians all made the mistake of believing that they could use Hitler for their own ends. Hitler was charismatic, and less popular politicians hoped that by allying themselves with Hitler they could rise to power with their Nazi allies. The two politicians most closely associated with this attempt to 'use' Hitler were von Papen and General von Schleicher. Von Papen made the following statement in 1932, memorable for its completely wrong assessment of the situation: 'In six months we'll have pushed Hitler so far into a corner he will be squealing.'

As a summary to an answer about Hitler's rise to power, you could say with confidence that, without the Great Depression, Hitler would have been unable to build up mass support. Nor would he have attracted the attention of right wing politicians who thought they could use him for their own ends.

In January 1933, Hitler was the Chancellor of a democratic government he despised. He was the leader of a coalition government in which the Nazis were a minority. So do not make the mistake of saying that Hitler was 'in power' by January 1933. You must be prepared to explain how Hitler went from legal Chancellor to legal dictator – in other words, what was the Nazi Revolution?

Germany 1815 – 1939

Section summary
In this section you should have learned:
- By 1932 some Weimar politicians were undermining the democratic system from within.
- By 1932 some Weimar politicians hoped to use Hitler to achieve their own antidemocratic ambitions.
- In January 1933 Hitler became Chancellor of Germany legally, within the Weimar Republic's Constitution.

Practise your skills

This section shows you how to plan an essay based on the question:

To what extent was discontent with the treaty of Versailles responsible for the rise of the Nazis to power?

Remember – topic and task!
Decide what the question is about (the topic) – this question is about why the Nazis rose to power.

Decide what you have to do (the task) – you must explain the importance of discontent with the treaty of Versailles as a reason for the rise of the Nazis but you must also show an awareness of other factors and consider them too.

Your beginning must outline what you will do. You could start by setting the context. Then mention anger and discontent about the Diktat treaty but do not develop this yet.

Then indicate the other reasons for the rise of the Nazis, including the weakness of the Weimar Republic. Use the sub headings in this section to help you understand and organise the main ideas, for example that Weimar politicians can be blamed for Hitler's rise and the collapse of Weimar

Republic and that Germans blamed the Weimar Republic for economic difficulties.

The middle

It is vital in the 'middle sections' of essays to show of your detailed knowledge. Don't waffle - be precise and accurate.

Explain more fully the points made in your introduction. Deal fully and in detail with the Treaty Of Versailles and the discontent that followed in one paragraph.

Then deal with each of the other reasons that you think explain the rise of the Nazis in one paragraph per main point.

Your conclusion :

A conclusion should have four main stages.

- The first stage is the first sentence where you restate the core issue of the question.
- The second phase could start *'on one hand .... and that introduces one side of your balanced conclusion.'*
- The third phase starts with *'On the other hand'* and there you present some evidence that *balances or counters your earlier evidence.'*
- Your final phase is where you weigh up your two sides and make your overall decision, perhaps starting with *'On balance ..''*

Example

In conclusion, the rise of the Nazis cannot be explained by looking at only one reason.

On one hand, negative reasons linked to the unpopular Weimar Republic made people look for alternatives.

On the other hand the positive attractions of Nazi promises attracted huge support.

On balance, the Treaty of Versailles was a continuing source of resentment and discontent that the Nazis exploited within their own policies that seemed so much more attractive than those of the tired and weak democratic parties.

Issue 6 – What methods were most successful in keeping the Nazis in power between 1933–1939?

The big picture

Between January 1933 and August 1934, Hitler took steps to move from being legal Chancellor in a democratic government to dictator of a totalitarian state. Democracy was destroyed, opposition was crushed and Hitler established a police state controlling the daily lives of German citizens by means of 'carrot and stick' methods. Propaganda, jobs and food along with a foreign policy that restored Germany's pride meant that many Germans supported him or at least did not complain. On the other hand, an atmosphere of fear reinforced by a secret police, and concentration camps for those who resisted, meant Nazi power went almost unchallenged between 1933 and 1939.

The destruction of democratic government

When the Nazis said they would hold their noses and enter the Reichstag they added 'sooner or later we will have power'. Hitler knew that the power of the Reichstag would have to be destroyed.

The Reichstag fire

In February 1933 the Reichstag caught fire. There is still debate about who started the fire but Hitler immediately put the blame on the Communists who were Hitler's main opposition. Hitler could claim that the communists had shown their anti-democratic ideas by burning the Reichstag. Hitler could then argue that Germany was under threat of a Communist Revolution and naturally, Article 48 could be used. The decree issued by Hitler (under the authority of the President) was called, 'for the protection of the People and State', but by banning many freedoms and allowing imprisonment without trial, Hitler was destroying democracy.

The Legal Dictatorship

Following the 'protection of the People and State', the Enabling Act authorised the Nazi-influenced government to issue laws that the Reichstag could not change. Even the signature of the President was no longer needed. The Enabling Act effectively killed Weimar democracy. The Nazis had established a legal dictatorship.

Centralising power

An authoritarian state can tolerate no challenge to its power. Very quickly Hitler made sure all German states were ruled directly from Berlin and the individual states had no separate political voice.

The removal of opposition

On July 14, 1933 the Nazi government declared the Nazi party to be the only legal political party in Germany. Without political choice there was no democracy. Trades unions were also banned by the Nazis because Hitler thought the unions might be centres of left-wing opposition.

From Dictator to Führer

Hitler still did not feel secure. Behind the scenes, Hitler needed the support of important groups of people – especially the army.

Hitler had already tried to link these powerful groups to the Nazis. In 1931 an alliance of right wing politicians, Junkers, senior army officers and the Nationalist ex-servicemen's association was formed. It was called the Hartzburg Front. This organisation helped Hitler with vital financial backing.

However, by 1934, the Nazi's private army, the SA, seemed to threaten Hitler's relationship with the army officers.

Some Germans loved Hitler. Some Germans hated him. Most Germans just accepted him. Do you think that explains how the Nazis stayed in power 1933-1939?

The Night of the Long Knives

The SA had caused much of the violence that disturbed Germany through the later 1920s and by 1934 Hitler saw them as at best an embarrassment, and at worst a threat to his security.

The leader of the SA was Ernst Rohm. He planned to merge the regular army with the poorly trained SA to make a people's army. The regular army were horrified and Hitler was worried. In any regime, support from the army is important. Hitler knew he had to choose between his old friends in the SA or the regular army officer class.

Hitler's elimination of the SA leadership happened on June 30, 1934. It was called 'The Night of the Long Knives'. Hitler's private bodyguards, the SS, were used to kill many of Hitler's enemies, including Rohm. The ruthless murder of suspected enemies made Hitler more secure and it pleased the regular army.

The Oath of Loyalty and the Death of Hindenburg

In August President Hindenburg died. The President had been the head of state and the guardian of the Constitution in Weimar Germany but when he died Hitler took on the role of President and Chancellor and merged them to become Führer. Earlier, Hitler had arranged for every individual member of the armed forces to take an oath of loyalty to Hitler personally. The result was that by August 1934 Hitler had complete power.

Section summary

In this section you should have learned:
- Hitler was aware that he needed to keep the right wing influential group in Germany 'on side'.
- The Night of the Long Knives helped to please the army.
- The oath of loyalty taken by the army was significant in the consolidation of Hitler's power.
- Hindenburg's death signalled the final end of the Weimar Constitution.

Practise your skills

How important was lack of opposition in Hitler's rise to dictatorship in 1934?

Remember - topic and task!

Decide what the question is about (the topic) – this essay is about how Hitler became dictator of Germany.

Decide what you have to do (the task) – you have to consider why there was such a lack of opposition and decide if that was significant in Hitler becoming dictator.

Your beginning must outline what you will do. You should indicate that while you know Hitler became Chancellor in 1933, real power was not achieved until 1934 – after the Enabling Act, the Night of the Long Knives the death of Hindenburg, the oath of loyalty and the creation of Hitler as Fuhrer. These events should only be touched on and explained more fully in the middle section of your essay.

You must also show you are aware that the split in the left wing parties and the lack of opposition from more moderate parties also played their part in Hitler's rise.

By laying out your intentions in the introduction you have made clear you understand the question and also the time scale you intend to cover.

The middle

You must deal fully with 'the legal revolution', how Hitler moved from being a minority Chancellor in January 1933 to Fuhrer by August 1934.

Why did no party or person try to stop him? What is meant by the legal revolution? Why was the left wing so divided. Was that split in the left really important? Or was the Nazi power machine just too strong? E.g. Nazi use of fear, arrest, censorship and the banning of opposition.

How easy was it to stop someone using the democratic constitutional process to destroy Weimar from within?

Your conclusion

A conclusion should have the four stages explained in previous 'practise your skills' sections.

> Example
>
> In conclusion, Hitler's rise to dictatorship cannot be explained by looking at only one reason.
>
> On one hand, a lack of opposition was an important factor. No group felt strong enough to stand up to the Nazis.
>
> On the other hand the Nazi machine was so powerful that by 1933/34 it was too late for any opposition to take action. After all the Nazis were rising legally within the democratic constitution. On balance, lack of opposition is always dangerous to any political system. In 1934 the Weimar Republic was destroyed by one strong party who took steps to make sure there was no opposition.

The Nazi police state

Nazi Germany was a police state. In a democratic society the police should not take sides in political arguments but in Nazi Germany the police were ordered to help the Nazis and persecute any opposition to them. Hitler had the power to make laws, to enforce the laws and to control the law courts.

Nazi Germany was a totalitarian police state that aimed at total control of all aspects of life in Germany.

In a democratic society, people should be free to belong to any organisation they choose, but in Nazi Germany opposition was not tolerated. Just after the Nazis came to power a civil servant resigned from his membership of an opposition party saying, 'I see no other solution but my resignation. The existence of my family is at stake.' Most non-Nazis in Germany believed that resistance was hopeless.

In a democratic society, judges are meant to make unbiased decisions. In Nazi Germany judges were told Nazi ideology was the basis for making any decisions.

In a democratic society citizens cannot be arrested unless they have broken a law that has been agreed by an elected parliament. In Nazi Germany people were kept in prison with no idea why they were there or when they would be released. Basic justice was denied to the German population.

Hitler deliberately unleashed a reign of terror with the intention of destroying all opposition and conditioning the rest of the population to obey. Although it is impossible to exaggerate the role of fear in the Nazi state the phrase 'carrot and stick' is sometimes used to explain the combination of coercion and fear (the stick) along with the provision of things people want (the carrot) as a means of explaining how the Nazis kept power.

> ### Section summary
> In this section you should have learned:
> - that the Nazis established a totalitarian police state
> - how the Nazis destroyed the system of justice, civil rights and individual freedoms.

The carrot and stick

The phrase carrot and stick comes from the saying that there are two ways to make a donkey move. One way is to use force and hit it with a stick. The other way is to encourage it to move by offering it attractive reasons to move, such as a carrot dangling just in front of its mouth.

The threat of the stick was undoubtedly used by the Nazis to make the population obey Nazi rules. However if threats and terror were 'the stick', it is also true to say that many people supported the Nazis because of the 'carrot'.

When considering the Nazi use of the 'carrot' in Germany you should deal with the following:

- Work and the economy
- Education and German youth
- Religion
- The use of propaganda
- Someone to blame for all Germany's problems
- A successful foreign policy that made Germany strong and internationally respected.

Germany 1815 – 1939

Work, leisure and the economy

When Hitler became Chancellor in 1933, unemployment stood at 25.9%. By 1939 it stood at less than 1%. Hitler had delivered his promise of providing work and bread for the German people. It is hardly surprising that many Germans who feared for their future saw Hitler as their saviour and willingly supported him.

The German Labour Front allowed workers to campaign for improved working conditions and gave workers access to the popular 'Strength through Joy' movement, which provided leisure activities for thousands of German workers.

Research suggests that Hitler's economic miracle was not really working by the later 1930s but by then was it possible to complain?

Education and German youth

The purpose of youth organisations, such as Hitler Youth and the League of German Maidens, was to prepare the boys for military service and the girls for motherhood. One member said, 'we were politically programmed' and that was a main aim of the Nazi education system. In schools German youth was indoctrinated with Nazi ideas.

Religion

Hitler believed that control of the churches was important to the maintenance of Nazi authority. As early as 1933 a Concordat or agreement was reached with the Catholic church, which meant that if the Church did not upset the regime the Church would be allowed to continue to preach in Germany. Protestant churches were put under the control of the Reichbishop, who only allowed church ministers who supported the Nazis to continue working.

The use of propaganda

Propaganda was vitally important for any regime trying to maintain control, spread its system of beliefs and to persuade the population to identify with the new regime. Recent research suggests that propaganda does not really persuade people to believe something they *do not want* to believe. For example, in this case educated middle class Germans accepted propaganda because it told them something they *wanted* to believe – that Hitler was saving Germany, especially from Communism.

Someone to blame

In Nazi Germany, Jews were visible targets who could be blamed for all of Germany's problems. According to Nazi propaganda, Germany had lost the Great War because of a Jewish, Communist conspiracy. According to the Nazis, Jews were also responsible for Germany's economic crises. Hitler offered a scapegoat, or an excuse, to explain Germany's problems and to help non-Jewish Germans feel better about themselves.

The removal of thousands of Jews from their jobs also created vacancies in the labour market, which could be filled by non-Jewish members of the master race. As unemployment fell, Hitler's popularity grew.

With no effective opposition, the Nazi persecution of Jews increased throughout the 1930s. However this book does not cover this Higher History option and finishes in 1939, the Final Solution and the gassing of millions of Jews did not begin until 1941.

Did most Germans support the Nazis?

As long as the pain of Nazi Germany did not affect most individuals in Germany, they were prepared to go along with the Nazis even if they did not agree with their actions or ideology. Drifting along with something while not actively approving or disapproving is called 'acquiescence'.

Most Germans were not active Nazis, but Nazism gave many Germans what they wanted. They were prepared to acquiesce as the Nazi dictatorship spread over all aspects of life in Germany in the 1930s and for most Germans life seemed better and more secure than in the 1920s.

Hitler's foreign policy also won him support in Germany

In 1919, Germany was humiliated by the Treaty of Versailles. The intention of the victors in the First World War was to keep Germany weakened so that it would never again threaten the peace of Europe. One of the attractions of the Nazi party was its promise to destroy the Treaty of Versailles and make Germany a strong and respected nation again. Between 1933 and 1939 Hitler became the dominant politician in Europe with strong foreign policy successes that made other countries look weak and afraid.

By 1935, Germany was rearming and in 1936 German troops moved into the demilitarised Rhineland. Germany could now reinforce its western border in preparation for changing the map of east-central Europe.

In 1938, Anschluss with Austria saw German power increasing and later that year Britain and France gave in to all Hitler's demands over Czechoslovakia in a desperate attempt to appease him and so avoid the risk of war.

In 1939, when German forces invaded Poland, Hitler had no reason to suspect that there would be any serious consequences.

Between 1933 and 1939 Hitler had restored the international power and status of Germany and the German public celebrated Nazi success.

Section summary

In this section you should have learned:
- that the Nazis extended their control to all sections of society and all areas of activity
- how the phrase 'carrot and stick' can be applied to Nazi control of Germany in the 1930s
- why most Germans accepted and even welcomed Nazi control over Germany.

Practise your skills

This section shows you how to plan an essay based on the question:

'The regime, after all, gave most Germans what they wanted.' How justified is this view of Nazi rule in Germany between 1933 and 1939?

Remember – topic and task!
Decide what the question is about (the topic) – this essay is about life in Nazi Germany between 1933 and 1939.

Decide what you have to do (the task) – the question offers you the 'carrot' view of how the Nazis maintained control over Germany between 1933 and 1939. You must decide if you agree with that view after weighing up the role of the 'stick'. In other words, how big a part did fear and force play in the Nazi control over Germany?

Essay advice
Introduction
The beginning must outline what you will do. Show that you intend to deal with the carrot and stick argument. How important was 'bread and circuses' to Nazi control and how big a part did fear and force play? Or is it possible that most Germans just acquiesced in Nazi policies and neither supported or opposed as long as their lives went on relatively unchanged and the Nazis delivered 'what they wanted'.

The middle
It is vital in the 'middle sections' of essays to showcase your detailed knowledge of Nazi policies and methods. Don't waffle – be precise and accurate.

There are two main sections to deal with. First of all show what you know about the 'positive' aspects of Nazi rule. What did they do that 'gave most Germans what they wanted'? The second section should deal with the use of force and terror – how far did the Nazis destroy opposition and use fear and force to guarantee support, or at least acquiescence?

Remember to start each paragraph with a key sentence that outlines the point you will be developing.

Your conclusion
In your conclusion you should:

- Decide whether or not you agree with the view expressed in the title. Make your decision clear.
- Sum up the differing points of view and prioritise what you think were the most important features of the Nazi regime within Germany.
- Try to include the word authority in an appropriate way and refer back to points in your answer where the Nazis were shown to maintain their authority in many different ways.

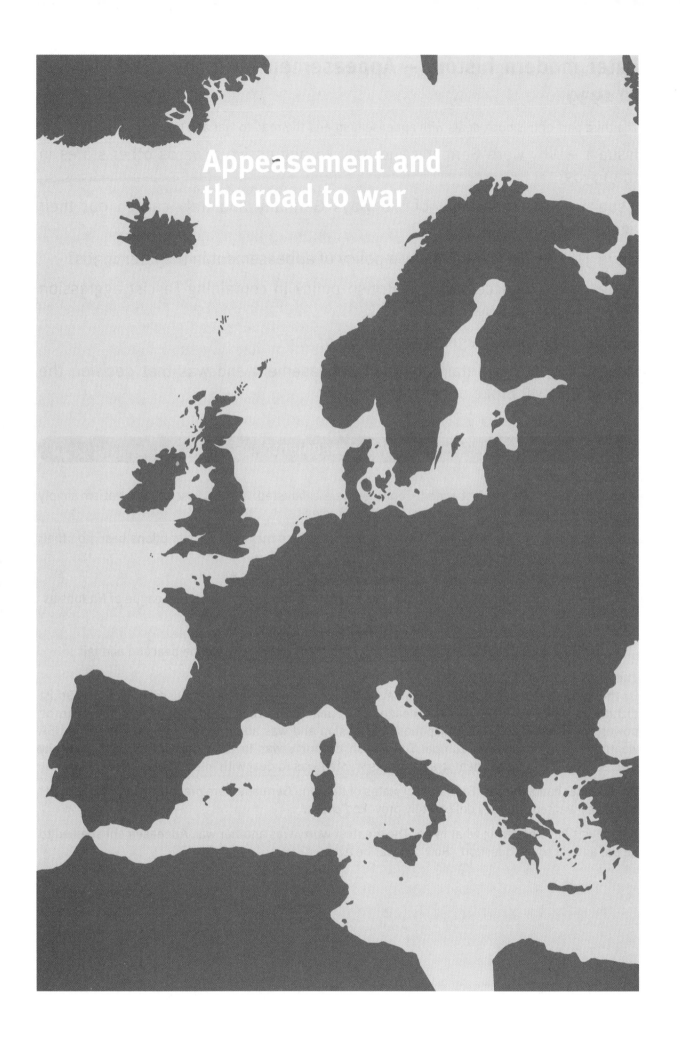

Appeasement and the road to war

Later modern history – Appeasement and the road to war, to 1939

The third part of this book deals with appeasement and the road to war and the six issues are:

Issue 1 – Why were Germany and Italy so aggressive towards other states in the 1930s?

Issue 2 – An assessment of the ways Germany and Italy carried out their aggressive policies.

Issue 3 – Why did Britain follow a policy of appeasement in the later 1930s?

Issue 4 – How successful was British policy in containing Fascist aggression between 1935 and March 1938?

Issue 5 – The Munich agreement – good or bad?

Issue 6 – Why did Britain abandon appeasement and was that decision the reason why war broke out in 1939?

Why appeasement?

The background

In 1919 the Great War had just ended. Countries were exhausted. In 1919, Fascism and Nazism simply did not exist. Mussolini and Hitler were almost unknown.

When the leaders of the victorious powers met at Versailles they made assumptions based on their experience and the world situation in 1919:

- They assumed that countries would be democratic and peaceful.
- They assumed the countries would help each other and support the new League of Nations as it would guarantee future peace.
- They believed that Germany should never again be able to cause trouble.
- They assumed that international relations between countries would be peaceful and fair.

These assumptions were wrong

By the early 1930s, democracy in Germany and Italy had been defeated. Mussolini was the fascist dictator of Italy and Hitler was Nazi leader of Germany. The League of Nations was shown to be powerless. It had failed to stop Japanese aggression and was about to fail with Italy too. The USA wanted nothing to do with Europe. The British economy was in ruins and France was politically divided. The last thing the democratic powers wanted was to deal with international crises.

On the other hand, the new Fascist/Nazi states of Italy and Germany were prepared to use force to get what they wanted and they deliberately provoked crises.

Britain was left wondering what to do. The greatest worry was another war. Appeasement seemed to be the answer to the question, 'How can war be avoided? '

Issue 1 – Why were Germany and Italy so aggressive in the 1930s?

The big picture
The aggressive nature of German and Italian foreign policy in the 1930s was the result of many influences. The Paris Peace Treaties left both Germany and Italy resentful and bitter. Both France and Britain were weakened by the war and fearful of another war. The League of Nations was created to maintain world peace but by the 1930s it was shown to be powerless. The rise of totalitarian dictatorships in Germany and Italy was also unexpected as was their willingness to use force to get what they wanted.

The Paris Peace settlements

The future of Germany was discussed and decided in the Palace of Versailles – hence the Treaty of Versailles. Austria was dealt with by the treaty of St Germain and Hungary was dealt with by the Treaty of Trianon – all palaces around Paris. The Paris Peace Settlement was meant to guarantee that there would never again be a war in Europe. However, the treaties pleased no one. Both Germany and Italy were left feeling bitter and wanting revenge.

The Treaty of Versailles
In 1919 the victorious allies made Germany sign the Treaty of Versailles. Germany was forced to accept blame for causing the war and all the death and destruction that resulted from it. Germany lost all colonies, much of its industrial resources and some areas of land. Tens of thousands of Germans found themselves living in new countries, such as Poland, created by the peace treaties.

Germany's armed forces were severely cut. Its army was cut to 100 000 men. No military aircraft, tanks or submarines were allowed.

Germany also had to pay compensation (reparations), to the victorious powers and to take the blame for all the damage and deaths caused by the war.

Most Germans were furious. They called the treaty a 'Diktat' – a dictated treaty that was forced on them.

Is there a connection between the Treaty of Versailles and the outbreak of World War Two?
There is no doubt that tensions created by the Treaty led to the Second World War 20 years later. The treaty provided a popular target for Hitler to attack during his rise to power.

France wanted to prevent any change in the treaty. Disagreements between France and Britain over how to deal with Germany prevented combined action.

Hitler could claim that his actions in the 1930s were merely demands for 'fair treatment' to balance the unfair treaty.

Italy and the Peace Treaties
When the war started in 1914, Italy had an alliance with Germany and Austria-Hungary. In 1915 Italy broke its promise and switched sides. Italy hoped to gain land from Austria-Hungary, especially in what is now Croatia and Slovenia, as a reward for being part of the winning side. When the peace treaties were signed Italy felt cheated and that it had not gained the rewards it hoped for. Italy was left embarrassed and wondering why they had fought in the war. When Mussolini came to power in 1922 he promised to make Italy great again and wipe out the embarrassment of the peace treaties.

The League of Nations

The League of Nations began its life on January 20, 1920 and was based in Geneva, Switzerland. Its purpose was to ensure world peace through a combination of disarmament and collective security. Both those methods failed.

The weakness of the League of Nations was a contributory factor to the outbreak of World War Two. The failure of the League also pushed Britain into finding a new way to secure peace.

Why did the League fail to prevent war?

The answer lies in weaknesses within the League and the unwillingness of its member states to support League policy. A main problem of the League was that it was not a League of all nations. The USA never joined, Germany and Russia joined for a short time later and aggressive nations simply left the League when the League criticized them.

Why did disarmament fail?

After the Great War there had been hopes that international disarmament would prevent war happening again but hopes for disarmament had collapsed by 1934.

Disarmament would only work if countries trusted each other but that was unlikely in the years following the Great War. One of the main obstacles to disarmament was the attitude of France. Throughout the 1920s and early 1930s the French attitude towards disarmament was summed up in the saying, 'France will not disarm physically until Germany disarms morally. '

By the mid 1920s, France planned a defensive and expensive policy based on a vast line of defences along the French/German border called the Maginot Line. It was meant to stop any German attack breaking into France.

France also made a series of alliances with central European countries such as Poland and Czechoslovakia. France wanted to encircle Germany by making alliances with East European countries that would help France if it was attacked. What France did not think about, was what would happen if Germany attacked the east European countries first!

On the other hand, Britain saw the French as being particularly unreasonable towards the Germans and refused to support French policy. Britain wanted to stay out of Europe as much as possible. That was bad news for the League because the League was only as strong as its strongest members – who just happened to be Britain and France.

In 1925, at the Treaty of Locarno, Germany accepted much of the Versailles settlement including the land losses to France and Belgium and the demilitarised Rhineland. It seemed as if a source of international bitterness had been solved. However, at Locarno, Germany said nothing about its eastern frontiers with Poland or Czechoslovakia and France remained suspicious about what Germany was planning in the east. Britain had made it clear that it was not very concerned about what happened in Eastern Europe. In such an atmosphere France was not likely to discuss disarmament.

By 1934, disarmament and the hopes of the League had faced serious set-backs. The democracies were weak and divided and the disarmament conferences failed to reach any agreement. Germany had left the League of Nations and Hitler had risen to power, promising to destroy the Treaty of Versailles. Britain hoped that by appeasing Hitler he might be tempted back in to the League. France was fearful of German growth and was against any appeasement of Germany.

Collective security failed to work

What was collective security?

The League had no army to enforce its decisions. Pressure from the League was only possible if member states agreed to join together to carry out the sanctions, or punishments, agreed by the League members. In other words, members of the League of Nations would have to work collectively to guarantee peace and security in the world. But what would happen if the main members of the League chose self-interest before collective security?

In the 1930s, collective security failed because members of the League of Nations were not prepared to get involved in issues beyond their own national interest.

Once the League's 'bluff' of collective security was called, it had no chance of preserving the peace. The weaknesses of the League were exposed in two crises – one in Manchuria and the other involving Abyssinia.

This cartoon is a comment from the early 1930s on the weakness of the League of Nations. The League is shown as a powerless rabbit hypnotized by the snake of International strife (trouble). The League is meant to stop strife. The cartoonist suggests that the league rabbit is about to be swallowed by the snake.

Manchuria, 1931

The first test of collective security came in 1931 when Manchuria was attacked by Japan. Manchuria was part of China and both China and Japan were League members who should obey League rules. The League failed to take strong action against Japan who went on to conquer more territory.

It is not necessary to know the details of the Japanese invasion of Manchuria for this course but it is important to be aware that the Manchurian crisis was the first test for the League – and the League failed.

Collective security had clearly failed to stop the attack or punish the aggressor.

Abyssinia, 1935

The Italian invasion of Abyssinia in 1935 was the second important test for collective security. Italy, a League member, attacked Abyssinia, another League member. Italy was condemned for its aggression but ignored the League. The main members of the League (Britain and France) failed to take strong action because they wanted Italy as a friend.

Once again the League failed to stop a country that was determined to use force to achieve its aims. The crisis also showed that Britain and France put self-interest before collective security.

By the mid 1930s, the League had failed and the failure of the League is linked closely to the adoption of the policy of appeasement by Britain.

The rise of dictatorships

World War Two would not have happened if Adolf Hitler had not become leader of Germany. As dictator of Germany he pushed forward an aggressive expansionist foreign policy aimed at making Germany great. To a lesser extent Mussolini tried the same thing for Italy.

The policy of appeasement is really the story of how Britain tried to deal with aggressive dictatorships.

What is a fascist dictatorship?

Before the Great War the idea of a political dictatorship was unknown. After the Great War, dictatorships spread across Europe.

For the purposes of this course, a fascist dictatorship is a country controlled by one man at the head of the only political party in that country. A dictator has total power and that helps to explain another phrase – **total**itarian dictatorship.

The rise of fascism in Italy

In Italy, public discontent with the democratic government also grew. The government was blamed for failing to gain much for Italy at the peace conference. It was blamed for failing to stop the wave of strikes and demonstrations that were hurting Italy's economy. Democratic politicians were blamed for doing private deals behind closed doors so that voters seldom got the government policies that they had voted for. The Italian people were simply fed up with weak government.

In 1922, Benito Mussolini became leader of Italy. His party was the fascist party and by 1925 he had made himself dictator – Il Duce – of Italy. At first Mussolini was hugely popular. He saved Italy from Communist Revolution – or so he said. He would make Italy strong powerful and feared by other countries – or so he said. Mussolini said it was better to live one day as a lion than a hundred years as a sheep. Italian foreign policy was aggressive.

The rise of Nazism in Germany

At the end of the First World War a new democratic government had been created in Germany called the Weimar Republic. The aim of the new republic was to govern Germany fairly and peacefully. However, a series of problems weakened the government and people became discontented with their new democracy.

In 1933, Adolf Hitler became leader of Germany. His party was the National Socialist German Workers party – or Nazi for short. By 1934 he had made himself dictator – Führer – of Germany. At first Hitler was hugely popular. He saved Germany from Communist Revolution – or so he said. He would make Germany strong, powerful and feared by other countries – or so he said. German foreign policy was aggressive.

Fascist ideology and foreign policy

'Foreign policy' means more than the way that Hitler and Mussolini dealt with other countries and how they tried to make their countries stronger.

As Hitler was by far the strongest of the two dictators, most of this course deals with Nazi foreign policy. It is also true that Hitler had a much more planned and detailed foreign policy, which was also linked to his fascist ideology.

You must have an understanding of what Hitler's foreign policy was in order to make sense of his moves between 1935 and 1939. Hitler's foreign policy was expansionist and potentially aggressive. It's hard to imagine how he could have achieved these aims without planning for war.

Nearly all Hitler's actions can be linked to four key aims, which he had outlined in his autobiography called *Mein Kampf*, written in the mid 1920s:

1. The Treaty of Versailles had to be destroyed. The treaty symbolised Germany's humiliation. Most of what happened later can be directly linked to Hitler's aim of destroying the Treaty of Versailles.
2. All German speaking people must live in one enlarged Germany. He said that all Germans had the right to live in Germany and if that meant the borders of Germany had to spread to take in extra Germans then he was prepared to make that happen. That would also mean that conflict with neighbouring countries was likely.
3. Germans were the master race. Hitler believed Aryans – or Germans – were the master race. Hitler talked about 'inferior' races such as Jews and Slavs as 'sub-humans' – not even real people. Hitler believed 'inferior races' had one purpose in life – to serve the master race.
4. Germany must have Lebensraum. Hitler believed that Germany was defeated in the Great War partly because it ran out of resources, especially food and oil. He claimed that Germany had to have all the land and resources it needed to survive and grow strong, even if it meant taking

these things from other countries. Hitler knew that the resources he wanted could be found in Russia. Most of Hitler's foreign policy was powered by his need for eastwards expansion towards and into Russia. This policy aim was called Lebensraum.

Was fascist aggression caused by economic difficulties after 1929?

In 1929 the US economy crashed. The recession that followed was exported worldwide. In Germany, unemployment reached six million, Hitler claimed he was Germany's last hope and that he could solve the economic problems. The economic crash is a vital part in understanding why Hitler came to power.

In Italy, Mussolini's economic policies were already showing signs of failure by 1929. In the 1930s, he relied on foreign policy adventures to distract the Italian people from the failures of his government. Mussolini also claimed that a new Italian Empire would bring everything from 'pineapples to platinum' to the Italian people.

In Japan, a new military dictatorship under the authority of the Emperor had seized power. The USA stopped buying Japanese silk and Japanese migrants could no longer escape to America to ease overcrowding. Where could Japan look for a solution to its difficulties? The answer lay in China. In Manchuria there was land and resources. Why not take them?

The answer to all the economic difficulties seemed to be aggressive foreign policies.

> ## Section summary
> Fascist ideology had several elements at its core. It wanted to change the Paris Peace Settlement, restore national pride, develop national empires and military strength, build up economic power and take resources as required from whoever had them.
>
> In contrast the democracies had their own problems. They were weak and indecisive – and there was no international organisation strong enough or united enough to challenge the new dictatorships.

> ## Practise your skills

This section shows you how to plan an essay based on the question:

How far was the Paris Peace settlement the reason for the aggressive nature of German and Italian foreign policy in the 1930s?

Remember – topic and task!

Decide what the question is about (the topic) – the essay title provides one possible explanation for the aggressive nature of German and Italian foreign policy in the 1930s. Do you agree with that view or should other reasons be considered? The question is really about *why* German and Italian foreign policy was so aggressive in the 1930s.

Decide what you have to do (the task) – you have to decide if the Paris Peace settlement was the real reason why German and Italian foreign policy in the 1930s was so aggressive or if other reasons were more important. You must demonstrate your knowledge about the other reasons and arrive eventually at a balanced conclusion.

Essay advice

Are there certain things that must be in an introduction?

Yes, it must have a sentence that suggests you are going to write a balanced essay by looking at all sides of the debate. You could do that by stating that the Paris Peace settlement was only one of many reasons. Then you should mention the other reasons but do not explain them yet. Remember this is your introduction.

In the 1930s, German and Italian foreign policy was very aggressive. The Paris Peace settlement had left both Germany and Italy unhappy and wanting to change the settlement (1). However, German and Italian foreign policy was also the result of new fascist dictatorships that led those countries.

All the assumptions of the early 1920s about peaceful democracies rejecting war were shown to be wrong with the rise of Hitler and Mussolini (2). These new dictatorships had ideologies that used aggression as deliberate policy (3). Economic difficulties after 1929 also made Germany and Italy look to aggressive military solutions to their problems (4). Finally the League of Nations that had been created to guarantee future peace and stability was shown to be powerless in the face of rising fascist aggression (5).

This a good introduction because the style is mature and clearly signposts the points to be raised in the essay. It provides a structure that the candidate can follow through the rest of the exam. There is no irrelevance and it is clear to an examiner that you have understood the question.

The middle

It should have five paragraphs, and each paragraph should be based on one of the five numbered points in your introduction. Each paragraph should contain relevant detailed knowledge that is used to explain why each of those points is relevant to an explanation of why fascist foreign policy was so aggressive.

Your conclusion

In the conclusion you must make your mind up and answer the main question. You should also sum up your main points. This can be a bit repetitive in that you will be mentioning again the main points made in your introduction.

To make your conclusion more effective, try to prioritise your reasons. This means you decide which of the many relevant points you raised in your introduction is the most important in the answer to the main question.

Never add more factual information into your conclusion. A conclusion ends your essay. It should not continue your essay or push it in a new direction by including new information.

A conclusion should have four main stages:

- The first stage is the first sentence where you state your main answer.
- The second stage could start, 'On one hand ...' and that introduces one side of your balanced conclusion.
- The third stage could start with, 'On the other hand ...' and there you present some evidence that balances or counters your earlier evidence.
- The final stage is where you weigh up your two sides and make your overall decision, perhaps starting with 'On balance ...'

Example

In conclusion, the aggressive nature of German and Italian foreign policy in the 1930s was the result of many influences. On one hand, the Paris Peace settlement was an important factor in providing German and Italian foreign policy with a focus and even some justifications for action. On the other hand, the political ideology of Nazi Germany and Fascist Italy and the lack of any organisation to stop it also explain the aggressive nature of the fascist regimes.

On balance, the Paris Peace settlement provided an easy target to complain about and convince the German and Italian people that their countries had been badly treated and that their new leaders would restore national pride by any means possible.

Issue 2 – An assessment of the methods used by Germany and Italy to pursue their foreign policies from 1933

> ## The big picture
> Between 1933 and 1939 the fascist powers of Germany and Italy used a combination of aggression and diplomacy to get what they wanted. Italy simply ignored the rules of the League of Nations when it attacked Abyssinia. When Hitler took action that broke the Versailles Treaty he usually claimed he was justified. Both dictators knew that Britain and France would do almost anything to avoid war. As time passed the balance of power tilted more in favour of the fascist powers. By the late 1930s, Germany, Italy and Japan were linked by alliances.

How did Hitler justify his actions?

In order to explain Hitler's tactics we will consider three domestic scenarios throughout this section that you might find familiar. They might also help in understanding the actions of Germany and Italy.

Scenario one

You have done something wrong. Your mother is angry. Just as she is about to give some punishment you say stop! It wasn't me. It was my brother/sister/friend. At that moment your mother is unsure what to do. Are you to blame? Are you telling the truth? Whatever happens next you have made your mother doubt herself. Should she punish you? Should she try to find out more? Either way, you have managed to delay punishment and if any punishment does head your way it will be less severe than her initial reaction.

How does this connect to Hitler's actions?

Hitler often claimed his actions were just self defence. Put like that, Britain found it difficult to take strong action against him.

In March 1935 Hitler announced to the world that Germany was rearming. Hitler claimed his actions were in self defence and if other countries would disarm then so would he. When Hitler walked out of the disarmament conference he blamed France for refusing to disarm and for remaining a threat to a weakened Germany. Hitler claimed he was only defending Germany:

> 'I say this to the leaders of Europe. Yes, we are breaking the treaty but we will get rid of our weapons immediately if other countries do the same. If we are allowed to defend ourselves then we offer a future of peace where all our differences can be discussed peacefully within the League of Nations without using force. But if you attack us we will resist to the last man!'

Scenario two

Your mother is unhappy about something you have done. You are about to be punished but before she does so, you make an offer. You suggest that if she lets you off just this once you will never do anything like it again. You also offer to do the household chores for the next six months and tasks that she has been nagging you about for a long time – such as revision.

She now has a difficult choice to make. If she punishes you for what you have done you will storm off in a bad mood. Nothing will get done around the house and you will not revise. You might then fail your exams and all her hopes for you will blow away. But if your mother accepts your offer all could be well!

How does this connect to Hitler's actions?

Hitler often said he had no more demands to make after what he had just done. He also suggested that if he was allowed to do what he had just done then Britain would benefit from it.

Hitler's remilitarisation of the Rhineland in March 1936 was his first major challenge to the stability of peace in Europe. It is also an example of scenario two. Here he used his excuses to get what he wanted.

The Rhineland was demilitarised as part of the Versailles Treaty. It meant that no German troops or military equipment was allowed on the side of the river Rhine nearest France. Nor were German troops allowed anywhere near the bridges over the Rhine.

The Rhineland was part of Germany and had not been taken away at the Versailles settlement. Be careful about that point – Hitler did not invade the Rhineland. Germany had not attacked anyone. The Rhineland was already part of Germany. On March 7th 1936 Hitler simply sent German soldiers back into it.

Why it was demilitarised?

A Rhineland with no German forces allowed in it meant that Germany could not launch a surprise attack on France or Belgium again. Check a map of the area to see why. It also meant that Germany's industrial heart – the Ruhr – was exposed to French attack if Germany was thought to be causing trouble. That was what happened in 1923 when French and Belgian troops invaded the Ruhr to force reparation payments from Germany.

Was the remilitarisation a gamble?

The League of Nations had been set up partly to supervise the terms of Versailles. As Britain and France were main members of the League, they should have taken action against Hitler. His military leaders had told Hitler not to remilitarise the Rhineland because the German army was in no position to fight if they had faced any opposition. Later, Hitler said he had ordered his forces to retreat if there was the slightest resistance. But he might have said that just to make his own actions look decisive and those of Britain and France weak. In any case, there was no resistance. Hitler's gamble paid off.

Why did Hitler need to remilitarise the Rhineland?

When Hitler remilitarised the Rhineland he claimed he was only doing so to protect Germany from attack on two fronts. In the 1920s, France had made a series of alliances with East European countries in an attempt to surround Germany. In February 1936, a new French–Russian alliance became 'live' and Hitler could claim he was under direct threat of a two-front attack.

Hitler knew that remilitarisation broke both the Treaty of Versailles and the Treaty of Locarno. At Locarno in 1926, Germany (then a democracy) had voluntarily accepted that the Rhineland would remain demilitarised. However, before Hitler started his eastwards expansion he needed a secure western frontier that he could defend.

Hitler knew France had a very strong defensive system, the Maginot Line. As soon as Hitler remilitarised the Rhineland he set about building the Siegfried Line – another strong defensive network. In effect, Hitler had closed his 'western back door'. Now he could advance eastwards knowing France would not attack a strong German frontier.

The German public and the military commanders were happy, Hitler felt politically safer and he could turn his attention to eastwards expansion and Lebensraum.

Why did Hitler get away with it?

The answer lies in the scenarios you have studied. Hitler had not attacked anyone and he could claim he was under threat. He also made an offer that Britain could not refuse!

In a speech just before remilitarization, Hitler offered to re-enter negotiations with Britain about disarmament and also the possibility of a new 25-year peace agreement. Hitler also suggested a new demilitarised zone involving French, Belgian and German territory. When he added to the package a new deal over the use of aircraft, and especially bombers, would it not have been foolish to reject his offers?

Later you will read that Britain and France were in no position to fight anyway – and by looking at scenario 3 you will discover there was no real cause to fight.

Scenario three

You go out on a Saturday night. You are told to be back by 1 am. You return at 2 am. Your mother is waiting up but nothing is said. Next week you have the same curfew but this time you are even later – 3 am. Once again your mother says nothing.

A few weeks later you come in at 1.10 am. Your mother explodes. She says you are late. You reply that you were much later the previous weeks so why get angry now? Your mother backs down. She has no justification to continue her fight with you.

How does this connect to Hitler's actions?

When Hitler moved troops into the Rhineland the treaty had already been broken or changed many times:

- In 1920, reparations were to continue without end. By 1930, reparations had been reduced and then eventually abandoned.
- In 1919, the German navy was severely reduced and no submarines were allowed. In 1935 the Anglo–German Naval treaty accepted the expansion of the German navy, including submarines.

When Hitler broke the Treaty of Versailles by remilitarising the Rhineland, or when he occupied Austria (Anschluss), or when he took the Sudetenland, it was hard for Britain to justify action on the basis of the Treaty of Versailles being broken. How could Britain justify war to defend a treaty that was already changed?

Spineless means weak. The cartoon shows Hitler walking all over the 'leaders of democracy'. Over their backs is a carpet, possibly a red carpet, suggesting Hitler is being treated far too well. They are shown bowing down to Hitler as he makes a rude gesture at them. One back has Rearmament on it. Another has Rhineland and Abyssinia. The other backs have question marks on them showing that no one knows where Hitler will strike next.

Fascist foreign policy 1935–39

In the section that follows you will see that both Germany and Italy used excuses, or justifications, to explain their actions or to minimise the reactions of Britain and France. Think how the scenarios described earlier can be used to help understand German and Italian action.

The crisis over Abyssinia

In October 1935, the Italian army invaded Abyssinia. Italy claimed its action in Abyssinia was to civilise a barbaric country. Mussolini argued that as Abyssinia was a League member it should apply League rules. The League was trying to stamp out slavery. Yet Abyssinia still accepted slavery in its country. Italy claimed it was helping to stop slavery, thereby supporting League of Nations policy.

In reality, Italy used the Abyssinian war to distract the Italian people from problems within Italy and to show off Italian power. Mussolini claimed he was rebuilding an empire in Africa.

Italy claimed huge victories in Abyssinia but critics of Mussolini pointed out that Abyssinian forces were poorly equipped and had no air defences – or aircraft!

From Mussolini's point of view, a victory in Abyssinia would show the world how powerful Italy had become under Fascist leadership. Mussolini also knew that Italian control of Abyssinia would be a threat to Britain's use of the Suez Canal as a route to Britain's imperial possessions in India and the Far East. That could be a useful tactical tool if ever a conflict arose with Britain.

The Abyssinian crisis also brought Germany and Italy closer together. Before the invasion of Abyssinia, Britain and France had seen Italy as a possible ally against Hitler. Mussolini did not like Hitler at first and when Hitler tried to invade Austria in 1934, Mussolini forced Hitler to back down. Britain and France were impressed and joined Italy in the Stresa Front, a loose alliance between the three countries aimed at restricting Hitler's moves and protecting Austria.

When Mussolini invaded Abyssinia, Britain and France were in a difficult position. They wanted to keep Italy as a friend but they also knew they should support the League. In December 1935, the newspapers revealed that Britain and France were trying to do a private deal with Mussolini that involved giving him most of Abyssinia. This private deal was called the 'Hoare Laval Plan', but it never happened. International complaints were so loud that the plan was abandoned. Mussolini was left annoyed with the criticism he got from Britain and France and he looked around for a new friend. He found Hitler only too happy to break up the Stresa Front.

The crisis over Spain

The Spanish Civil War lasted from 1936 until 1939. It was fought between the Republicans who represented the legitimate, elected government of Spain and the Nationalists who were trying to overthrow the government. The Nationalists were led by General Franco.

The war started because of tensions in Spain but the international importance of the civil war lies in how it was affected by the actions, or lack of action, of the major European powers.

In the end the Nationalists won. A major reason was the help they received from Germany and Italy while the Republicans got very little outside help. Germany and Italy claimed the elected government (the Republic) was only a cover for the creation of a communist government in Spain. Therefore Germany and Italy claimed they only got involved in the civil war to stop the spread of Communism.

In reality, Hitler used the Spanish Civil War as a testing ground for his air force, code named the 'Condor Legion'. German military planners could use Spain as a practice ground for tactics, communications and co-ordinating air, artillery and infantry attacks.

Later, Hitler's *Blitzkrieg* – or lightning war – attack into western Europe in 1940 used tactics developed in the Spanish Civil War.

Hitler also hoped for an alliance with the new Spanish dictator Franco and perhaps to gain access to Spain's raw materials, especially tin and iron.

Italy used the war to show off Italian strength and to gain naval bases in the Spanish Balearic islands – Majorca, Ibiza and Minorca.

The crisis over Austria, March 1938

In March 1938, German troops marched into Austria, against the rules of the Treaty of Versailles. That event was called the 'Anschluss', which means the joining together of Austria and Germany. Germany successfully absorbed Austria into the German Reich and took another important step eastwards.

How did Anschluss fit in with Hitler's foreign policy aims?

Hitler wanted to create a 'Greater Germany' by linking German speaking people together. He wanted to break the Treaty of Versailles and start spreading east as part of his Lebensraum plan. (But be careful – don't think that he wanted Austria for Lebensraum. Austria was just a stepping stone to that target.)

The changing balance of power

Hitler had already tried to take over Austria in 1934 but he had been blocked by Mussolini. The Italian leader threatened to send troops into Austria to prevent Germany taking it over. At that time Mussolini was not a friend of Hitler. Britain and France saw Mussolini as a potential ally against Hitler and that explains why they were unwilling to take action against Mussolini when he attacked Abyssinia in 1935.

However, after falling out with Britain and France over the Abyssinian crisis and helping the Nationalist side in the Spanish Civil War, Mussolini became friendlier with Hitler. The balance of power shifted, which meant that Germany was stronger, Britain and France were weaker and Austria was at the mercy of Germany.

Preparations for Anschluss

Between 1934 and 1938, the Nazis kept up the pressure on Austria, most of which was organised by an Austrian Nazi called Arthur Seyss-Inquhart whose task was to prepare for a Nazi takeover.

The use of Seyss-Inquhart shows another tactic used by Hitler. In Austria and later in Czechoslovakia, Hitler used Nazi supporters inside those countries to cause trouble and destabilise the governments. When German troops marched into Austria, Hitler claimed they were only moving in to help stabilise the country from communist troubles. He also pointed to the tens of thousands in the cheering crowds who welcomed the Germans. He argued that Austrian Germans were destined to be part of his Greater Germany. He also argued that the Austrians had been denied a fair and free choice about their future at the Paris Peace Treaties. Why should the German speaking Austrians not be part of a German Empire? Once again Hitler was using excuses and justifications to confuse international reaction.

In reality, Hitler's aim was to spread eastwards into Russia and seize the land for Lebensraum. To get there he must have access through Austria and Czechoslovakia. Once Austria was taken then Czechoslovakia was in a very vulnerable position.

Agreements, pacts and alliances

By 1939 Hitler had allied himself to two other strong powers, both of which would be very useful to Hitler's future plans.

On 21 October 1936, Germany and Italy signed a formal alliance which came to be known as the 'Rome–Berlin Axis'. Mussolini declared that the two countries would form an 'axis' around which the other states of Europe would revolve. Later, in May 1939, Italy and Germany formed a full alliance, called by Mussolini the 'Pact of Steel'.

Hitler also made an alliance with Japan. At first glance it seems strange that Nazi Germany should involve itself in the Far East – but that was not Hitler's intention. The secret to understanding the alliance with Japan is to think of Russia. Russia is huge. Hitler was on the western side of Russia, but further around the globe Japan was at Russia's eastern edge.

By the early 1930s, Japan was looking for friends. Its old alliance with Britain had ended and the USA was unfriendly. Japan's military dictatorship was unlikely to find friends in any democratic state and Japan was also afraid of the might of Communist Russia, an old enemy of Japan. Japan was only too happy when Hitler suggested an alliance.

On 25 November 1936, Japan and Germany signed the Anti-Comintern Pact. Since 'anti' means against and a 'pact' is an agreement and Comintern was short for Communist International, the anti-Comintern Pact was an agreement to stop the spread of Communism. In reality it put Russia in a sandwich between Germany and Japan. In any future conflict Russia would have to fight Germany on one front and Japan on the other. From Germany's point of view the agreement would prevent Russia targeting all its resources against Germany. Japan gained a similar advantage. By the end of 1936 the game of international alliances and strategy had become global. Italy joined the pact in 1937 and the possibility of a three-front war in Europe, the Mediterranean and in the Far East that haunted Britain was becoming more likely.

By the late 1930s, the balance of power was strongly in favour of Hitler, and the realisation that Britain was in an increasingly weak position influenced Britain's policy of appeasement, as you will see in Issue 3.

Practise your skills

This section shows you how to plan an essay based on the question:

How successfully did Germany pursue its foreign policy between 1933 and 1938?

Essay advice

Introduction

Your introduction must outline what you will do. This question asks 'how successfully' and you can only judge success against what Hitler wanted to achieve. In this essay you must establish what

Germany's foreign policy aims. Once you have done that you have a structure in your essay and you can use your factual knowledge to develop the main themes.

> ### Example
>
> German foreign policy between 1933 and 1938 was largely based around Hitler's aims outlined in *Mein Kampf*. His first aim was to destroy the terms of the Treaty of Versailles (1). His second was to create a Greater Germany including all German speaking people (2). Another Nazi aim was to achieve Lebensraum for Germany and that was to be found in Russia and Eastern Europe (3). Finally, Nazi ideology was racist and within his foreign policy Hitler wanted to establish the power of the Aryan master race over the inferior peoples of Eastern Europe (4).

The middle

You now have an introduction that leads into four paragraphs. In each paragraph you must do two main things. The first is to show your detailed knowledge. The second is to include analysis, and that means you must comment on how successful Hitler was in achieving each aim.

The information that should be in paragraph one should include:
- German rearmament
- remilitarisation of the Rhineland
- the Anglo-German Naval Treaty
- German forces in Spain to rehearse
- Anschluss

You should recognise that achieving those targets all did something to break or revise the Treaty of Versailles, and that was the first aim mentioned in the sample introduction.

For analysis, you should mention the strategy that Hitler employed to achieve his aims, such as the offers he made just before remilitarisation. You should also include that he did in fact achieve those aims so clearly that he was successful in this area.

Go on to develop three more paragraphs in the style just outlined.

Your conclusion

Finally you must have a conclusion. Your conclusion should answer the main question.

Start by writing, '*In conclusion …*' and write one sentence that makes a general answer to the main question such as, '*In conclusion Hitler was very successful in his foreign policy between 1933 and March 1938.*'

Then write, '*On one hand …*' and summarise your information that supports one point of view about the essay title such as, '*On one hand many of his aims had been achieved by March 1938.*'

Then write, '*On the other hand …*' and here you must sum up the evidence that gives a different point of view about the main question such as, '*On the other hand Hitler had not been successful in his first attempt at Anschluss in 1934 and by March 1938 he had not yet secured a clear path to Lebensraum in the east.* '

Finally write, '*Overall …*' and then write an overall answer to the main question, such as, '*Overall, Germany pursued its foreign policy between 1933 and March 1938 very successfully. However, after March 1938 the pursuit of the same foreign policy was to lead Germany to war and eventual defeat. But that was in the future and in March 1938 Nazi power dominated or scared the rest of Europe.* '

Issue 3 – Why did Britain adopt the policy of appeasement?

> ## The big picture
> Even now the word appeasement suggests something bad or weak. Critics of appeasement say that Britain was just giving in to bullies in the 1930s. Recent research however shows that there are many sensible reasons to explain why Britain adopted a policy of appeasement in the 1930s.

In the 1950s and 1960s the policy of appeasement was condemned as a policy of cowardice and foolishness. In the early 1940s, a book called *The Guilty Men* was published. The book blamed politicians who supported appeasement for helping to cause World War Two. The 'guilty men' argument is easy to summarise – clearly World War Two was caused by Hitler, but if Hitler had been stopped at an earlier stage the war would have been prevented. Therefore, those politicians who did not support Hitler must be partly responsible for the war. But hindsight is a wonderful thing to have!

You have already found out that Hitler used excuses and justifications to confuse and delay international reaction to his actions. So stopping Hitler would not have been as easy or as clear cut as the later anti-appeasers made out.

Then something happened in 1967. Before that date all official government papers were kept private for 50 years. In 1967 the 50-year rule was reduced to 30 years and suddenly historians had access to all the official government papers about appeasement.

Once these documents were studied it became clear that Chamberlain and others had very specific reasons for developing the policy of appeasement. Far from a policy of cowardice, appeasement became a policy with very clear reasons and justifications.

What were the reasons for appeasement?

Economic concerns

As early as 1934, the British government was getting warnings from the Committee of Imperial Defence (C.I.D.) that Hitler was 'the ultimate potential enemy'. At that time, Chamberlain was Chancellor of the Exchequer in charge of Britain's economy. Britain was in a depression. He knew that jobs and better housing were priorities for the British public. The public had votes and Chamberlain knew the public would not support large scale military spending. They wanted 'butter before guns '.

By 1937, the military balance of power was worse for Britain and Britain's economy was still weak. Without military resources was there an alternative to appeasement?

Attitudes to the Paris Peace Settlement

As you know, much of what Hitler did in the 1930s broke the Treaty of Versailles. But was that a reason to go to war? You have already read that the Treaty had been altered many times before 1936 so why not allow some more changes? Put simply, most of the British public felt the Treaty of Versailles was too harsh on Germany anyway. When it was first drawn up in 1919 people wanted revenge on Germany. As years passed, the public realised that the Treaty had been unreasonable and unrealistic. Could politicians really justify fighting again to defend the Treaty? What had Hitler done anyway? Between 1936 and 1938, Hitler attacked no one. In 1935 Britain even negotiated a change in the treaty with the Anglo–German Naval Agreement. In 1936, he moved troops 'in his own back garden'. In 1937, no British politician was prepared to confront Hitler over his actions in Spain. In March 1938, German troops were welcomed into Austria. What was there to fight about?

Public opinion and pacifism

Unlike the fascist dictators, British leaders had to think about public opinion. In 1918, all men over 21 had gained the right to vote and after 1928 so had women. By the mid 1930s, the British electorate was huge compared to only 20 years before – and it was clear to all politicians in Britain that the vast majority of the public were opposed to war.

In 1918, the public were told they had fought 'the war to end all wars'. In the 1920s thousands of war memorials across Britain were built. Public grief at the losses of the Great War was still huge. Could any politician suggest a policy that would cause the children of the soldiers of the Great War, now entering their late teens, to be sent to war again?

The British public was anti-war for two main reasons. One reason looked to the past, the other looked to the future:

- The past – the horrors of the Great War were still fresh in the minds of the public. The writings of the war poets, anti-war films of the early 1930s and the annual remembrance services all reminded the public that war must never happen again.
- The future – by the mid 1930s everyone knew, 'The bomber will always get through.' In the cinemas, newsreels showed Spanish cities wrecked by bombing and Abyssinians burned by chemical weapons dropped by Italian planes. Blockbuster movies such as *Things to come* predicted a war starting in 1940 in which wave after wave of bombers would destroy British cities. The government and public were terrified of bombing. For the first time British cities would be in the front line of enemy attack. That must not be allowed to happen.

Pacifism

Pacifism means fear of war and the desire to avoid conflict at any cost. By the early 1930s, anti-war movements were growing in Britain. Be careful of claiming that all of public opinion supported appeasement. It did not.

In 1933, the Co-operative Women's Guild produced the first white poppies to be worn on Armistice Day. They believed the red poppies were too linked to war and militarism. They wanted to mark the sacrifice of their husbands, sons and fathers – but they saw military spending across Europe rising. They were more disillusioned with promises that war had been ended rather than supporters of pacifism.

Historians sometimes use the 1933 East Fulham by-election as evidence for pacifism. A Labour candidate supporting disarmament and collective security won by nearly 5000 votes, overturning a previous Conservative majority of 14 000. However, most voters were much more concerned about housing and unemployment.

More shockingly for some people, an Oxford University Union debate voted 275 to 153 in favour of the motion, 'That this House will in no circumstances fight for its King and Country.' But were those students representative of the public?

By 1936, support for pacifism was at its height. The Peace Pledge Union gained 11 million signatures against war. But was that support for pacifism? Public opinion polls found that the most favoured foreign policy in the late 1930s was not appeasement but support for the League of Nations and collective security. By December 1937, 72% of people interviewed still expressed support for the League. In March 1938, a poll asked, 'Do you support Mr Chamberlain's foreign policy?' 58% said 'no' with only 26% saying 'yes'. Clearly the public was concerned about the danger of war – but be careful not to assume that meant support for appeasement. What is true is that the mass media, especially newsreels and radio, were carefully managed by the government to give an impression of support for appeasement.

Concern over the Empire

The British Empire was huge. It could truthfully be said that 'the sun never sets on the British Empire'. The Empire stretched around the world and there would always be some place in the empire where the clock showed twelve noon. One-quarter of the world's population was under British rule and it was the wealth and power that came with the Empire that made Britain into a world power.

Defence of the Empire was Britain's number one concern. The government department that advised the government on Empire matters was called the 'Committee of Imperial Defence'. As early as 1934 the C.I.D. had warned the government that Britain could not fight a war on three fronts. If Britain became involved in a war in Europe, would Japan start to nibble at the Far East and would Mussolini target the Middle East? The route through the Suez Canal was vital to Britain's global communications. Close to the Suez Canal was Palestine. Mussolini was already stirring up an Arab revolt in Palestine that was tying down over 10 000 British troops. The British army was overstretched.

Another concern was Empire unity. In the Great War, Empire troops from around the world fought for Britain. Would they do the same again? What relevance was a European war to New Zealand, Australia or South Africa?

At an Empire conference in 1937 the South African Prime Minister, Herzog, had said that if Britain became involved in a war with Germany, South Africa would not feel it had to help. Would the rest of the Empire follow that lead and refuse to help?

Britain had no reliable allies

By the late 1930s Germany, Italy and Japan were allied together but Britain had no allies apart from the Empire – and that was causing concern. Chamberlain knew he could expect no help from the isolationist USA. In a private letter to his sister, he had written, 'You can count on the Americans for nothing but words.'

France was the only other country that might help Britain but France had its own problems. In 1934, street rioting had brought down the government. France was politically divided and no short-term leader would commit France to any warlike moves against Germany. Anyway, was France not safe behind its expensive Maginot Line? The problem with that was the Maginot Line could not move. If French troops had to take action against Germany they would have to move out of the Maginot Line. That was politically difficult to do, especially as France was worried about the promises it had made to Eastern Europe in the 1920s.

Fear of Communism

A common saying at the time was, 'better Hitlerism than Communism'. What was the point of fighting Nazism if the result was that Communists came to power in European countries?

Many in Britain thought Hitler had brought strong stable government to Germany. The big political fear for Europe in the 1930s was Communism. Communism promised the destruction of European economies and governments. If Hitler was overthrown, who or what would replace him? Hitler's main challenger had been Communism. The thought of Communism spreading in Europe horrified British politicians. That fear was one of the main reasons Britain refused to support the elected government of Spain during the Spanish Civil War – it had communists in it!

Military weakness

If Britain had decided to stop Hitler by military action the question would have been asked: 'With what will we fight? '

Britain had disarmed hugely at the end of the Great War. Out of 130 000 serving aircraft at the end of the war only 120 were still in use three years later. Britain had adopted the 10-year rule, partly to save money. The belief was that any possible threat to Britain would be easily spotted and Britain would have plenty of time to get ready. Wrong!

The arrival of fascist military dictatorships in the 1930s took British military planners entirely by surprise. The heads of Britain's armed forces – the Chiefs of Staff – had consistently warned Chamberlain that Britain was too weak to fight. At the same time, Hitler's propaganda encouraged Britain and France to believe that Nazi forces were stronger than they really were. Nazi film of soldiers marching into the Rhineland hid the fact that the soldiers were raw conscripts barely able to march in straight lines. Nazi tanks shown at rallies were often cardboard outlines placed over ordinary cars. But at the time British politicians did not know that. The fighter planes and radar that saved Britain from defeat in 1940 were still at the development stage in the late 1930s. Britain needed time to rearm.

Why did Chamberlain choose appeasement?

Strong anti war public opinion in GB

The League was ineffective

Protect the empire

It is not a vital British interest

Rearmament was very expensive

Was France being provocative?

The British Empire might not help

The Germans were badly treated after the Great War

Britain had no firm alliance to protect central Europe

Britain had too many possible enemies

Britain had no allies

Hitler was a realistic politician. He would even stop making demands

The British armed forces were not ready

Political opposition to rearmament

Fear of communism

Committee of Imperial Defence said protection of the Empire was Britain's top priority.

Fear of war

Chiefs of Staff said Britain could not fight a war and win it.

Chamberlain was not fooled by Hitler. He knew the problems facing Britain and also that there was no choice but somehow to deal with Hitler.

Chamberlain's own beliefs

Chamberlain was a man who thought he could maintain peace in Europe. He was a very able and ambitious politician. He even combined the job of Prime Minister with Foreign Secretary in the late 1930s. Some critics say Chamberlain was fooled by Hitler. But was he?

At the Munich meeting, Chamberlain made it clear to his assistants that he did not trust Hitler. He pointed out that one must deal with the leader that exists, not the leader one would like to meet. Hitler had to be dealt with, not wished away. Hitler was also unique, there had never been a leader like him in modern times. At first he seemed reasonable. Everyone knew that in negotiations big claims must be made and eventually compromises can be made. Hitler needed to talk big to keep support at home, please his army and gain international respect. What surprised everyone was that Hitler was utterly without principle, would break promises when it suited him and meant what he said!

Given those circumstances could Chamberlain have done anything else? Chamberlain himself seemed surprised that conflict involving Britain could have grown out of issues that did not concern Britain: 'How horrible that we should be trying on gas masks because of a quarrel in a far away country between people about whom we know nothing.'

To appease or not to appease?

So, with all those issues in your mind – just as they were in Chamberlain's mind when he flew to meet Hitler – what would you have done? Do you think it was a policy of cowardice and foolishness? Or was appeasement a rational response to the situation confronting Britain in the 1930s?

Appeasement and the road to war

This section shows you how to plan an essay based on the question:

How far was pressure from public opinion the reason why Britain adopted a policy of appeasement?

Remember – topic and task!

Decide what the question is about (the topic). This essay is called 'an isolated factor' essay. The essay title provides one possible reason why appeasement became British policy and you are asked if you agree with that view or whether other reasons should be considered. You have to decide if public opinion was the real reason why appeasement became British policy or if other reasons were more important.

Decide what you have to do (the task) – perhaps start by saying public opinion 'partly' explains why appeasement became policy. Then you must argue there were other influences on the government. Your essay should explain and show off what you know and develop each of the influences on the government before reaching a conclusion.

Essay advice

Introduction

Here is an example of a very weak introduction:

> In order to answer this question it is necessary to explain why appeasement happened and decide if public opinion was a main reason. Appeasement encouraged Hitler and led to World War Two.

- It is far too short – only two sentences long.
- This introduction does nothing to help the writer. Time is wasted by almost writing out the question. All it does is pretend to be an introduction.
- There is no thought here about how the essay will develop.
- There is no sign posting of any ideas about why the reforms happened.
- The second sentence is completely irrelevant by writing about the link between appeasement and World War Two.

Here is a much better introduction:

> By the mid 1930s the government was concerned about growing fascist power in Germany and Italy. Public opinion was very anti-war and that was one influence on the government when they adopted the policy of appeasement. Other reasons such as a lack of reliable allies (2) and worries about support from the Empire (3) also played a part in that decision. Britain also had Economic concerns (4) and a fear that if Nazism was defeated then Communism would fill the gap (5). On a very practical level, Britain was concerned that its army was too weak to fight (6) so appeasement was the only option. It was also felt that the Paris Peace Settlement was too harsh and a policy of appeasement would allow for revision of the harsher parts of the treaty (7).

This is a better introduction because:

- The style is mature and signposts clearly the points to be raised in the essay. If it helps, there is no reason why you cannot faintly number your separate points with a pencil as a guide to yourself what the main development paragraphs should be about.
- It provides a structure that the candidate can follow through the rest of the exam.
- There is no irrelevance and it is clear to an examiner that you have understood the question.

The middle

This section should have seven paragraphs, one for each of your numbered points in the introduction. Each paragraph should contain detailed, relevant knowledge and also show how important you think the point of the paragraph was in persuading the government to adopt appeasement.

Your conclusion

Your conclusion is as important as all the other sections in your essay. Unless you have a suitable conclusion, you are likely to gain less than half marks. A suitable conclusion is a paragraph at the end of your essay that makes clear you are summing up your essay and providing a final overall answer to the question set. It should last about five or six lines of text and preferably start with words such as 'Finally' or 'In conclusion'.

What makes a good conclusion?

Throughout your essay you should have been arguing a case and weighing up different reasons to explain why appeasement happened. You would explain why public opinion was an important reason but you would also have considered other reasons. In your conclusion you would have to make your mind up and answer the main question.

Here are three examples of possible conclusions.

This is a weak conclusion:

> Appeasement happened because the politicians were concerned about public opinion. Fear of bombing caused the government to use appeasement and it helped keep the peace and avoid war.

Why is this a weak conclusion?

It is weak because it does not make clear it is a conclusion. There is neither balance here in summing up the other reasons, nor any attempt to decide which were the most important reasons. There is also a big error. Ultimately appeasement did not prevent war!

Here is a better conclusion:

> In conclusion, the policy of appeasement was a result of many issues. Pressure from public opinion was one of them. There were also worries from other reasons like fear from the empire, the spread of communism and also a feeling that the Treaty of Versailles had been too harsh.

This is a better conclusion, but not a good one. It starts by making clear this is the conclusion. It sums up some points that have been developed earlier in the essay but they are presented as a list rather than a balanced conclusion.

Here is a good conclusion:

> In conclusion, the policy of appeasement was the result of many pressures on the government. On one hand, pressure from public opinion was an important influence on a government dependant on votes. On the other hand, concern over Empire unity and the cost of rearming were major headaches to the government. They also felt the treaty of Versailles should be revised and with fear of war so high in people's minds it was felt negotiation would resolve differences far easier than conflict.
>
> On balance, public opinion was an important factor as it covered so many issues and, combined with Britain's lack of readiness to fight and lack of strong allies, perhaps appeasement was the only possible policy to follow at the time.

This is a very good conclusion because it meets all the requirements:

- It is clearly marked as the conclusion.
- It sums up the main issues developed in the essay. At the same time, it prioritises the reasons and suggests that the policy was inevitable because of all the pressures.
- Finally the quality of written English, the vocabulary, the awareness of essay structure and an argued case puts this well into the A pass category.

Issue 4 – How successful was British foreign policy in containing fascist aggression between 1935–38?

The big picture

Britain did avoid becoming involved in a major European war at this time. On the other hand, critics of British policy have argued that all Britain did was to encourage Hitler to demand more and more. Britain participated in the breaking of the Versailles Treaty and the Naval Treaty. Self-interest dominated British policy over Abyssinia and, in Spain, Britain was prepared to see a democratically elected government be overthrown by a fascist dictator. Finally, Britain did nothing to protect Austria from Nazi takeover but realists argued what could Britain have done?

Britain had several aims when dealing with fascist aggression. These were:

- to avoid war
- to seek ways of removing grievances
- to use negotiation to reduce international tension
- to protect the Empire
- to try as far as possible to work within the League of Nations
- to seek ways to promote disarmament

All of these aims can be seen running through British actions between 1935 and 1938. The first example of containing fascist aggression came with Italy's attack on Abyssinia.

The Crisis over Abyssinia

When Mussolini launched his invasion of Abyssinia, Britain was faced with a problem. Should it stand by the rules of the League and protect Abyssinia, or was it more important to keep Italy 'on side' as an ally against Hitler?

Self-interest or collective security?

Mussolini had made it clear that any action taken against Italy, especially stopping supplies of oil, would be seen as an act of war. Britain's military leaders believed that Britain could not defeat Italy quickly. More importantly, any conflict in the Mediterranean Sea area would threaten Britain's route to its Empire in India and the Far East.

According to the League Covenant (its rules), Italy should be punished for attacking Abyssinia and Britain, as a League member, should take action to stop Italy as part of the collective security arrangements. On the other hand Britain saw Italy as an important ally against Germany. Just a few months before Britain, France and Italy had joined the Stresa Front against future German expansion.

The Hoare–Laval Plan

Britain and France were in a difficult position. Their solution was the Hoare–Laval Plan, which was intended to 'buy off' Italy with the offer of territory in northeast Africa, some of it Abyssinian, on condition Italy stopped its war. It looked as Italy was about to be rewarded for its aggression.

To make matters worse, the Hoare–Laval Plan was leaked to the newspapers before the idea of giving in to Italy had been 'sold ' to the public. When details of the plan were published by the press in December 1935 there was a big scandal. Britain and France were accused of 'selling out ' League principles and putting self-interest before their League obligations.

The Hoare–Laval plan was an attempt to stop the war and avoid alienating Italy. However, collective security was abandoned, fascist aggression seemed to be accepted and a League member was not supported, all because of self-interest.

The Hoare Laval Plan was the first big sign of appeasement in action.

Many historians consider the crisis over Abyssinia to be the rock on which the League was wrecked. As A.J.P. Taylor wrote in *The Origins of the Second World War*:

> 'The real death of the League was in December 1935. One day it was a powerful body imposing sanctions; the next it was an empty sham, everyone scuttling from it as quickly as possible. '

Can Britain claim any success in its handling of the crisis?

No, it can't. The League was shown to be weak. Abyssinia was not saved. Italy continued its attack until Abyssinia was defeated.

Britain and France were shown to be unreliable and deceitful when the Hoare Laval plan was leaked.

The balance of power shifted against Britain.

Hitler was encouraged. Mussolini and Hitler drifted closer together and finally Britain now had an enemy in the Mediterranean. In future dealings with Hitler, Britain still had to consider the possibility of conflict with Italy at the same time.

German rearmament and the Anglo–German Naval Treaty

How did Britain react to German rearmament?

Opinion in Britain was divided about what to do. On one hand, some people such as Winston Churchill argued that Hitler was 'moving Germany along the path of war again.'

On the other hand, realists in the British government asked what could we do about it? Hitler made a case to justify rearmament while in Britain the terms of the Treaty of Versailles were now seen as far too harsh and therefore open too change.

The Anglo-German Naval Agreement, June 1935

The Treaty of Versailles had severely cut the size of the German navy. The treaty had clearly stated that Germany was only allowed six large warships and no submarines. It can be argued that Britain encouraged further German rearmament when the Anglo–German Naval Treaty was agreed in June 1935. The new treaty accepted that Germany should have a navy up to one-third the size of the British navy and Germany was allowed to build submarines!

Could Britain claim the naval treaty was a success for its policy?

The British government believed that Nazi Germany would develop her navy regardless and that an official agreement between Nazi Germany and Britain would do a lot to improve relations between Britain and Germany.

There was also a feeling in some quarters in Britain, that the Treaty of Versailles had been too harsh on Germany and that the time was right to revise some of the harsher terms.

Britain hoped that by negotiation and revising the treaty that Nazi Germany would have no reason to be angered or feel cornered by the old terms of Versailles.

One argument in favour of the Treaty was that if Nazi Germany kept the 1935 Agreement, Britain would have a very good idea of the size of Germany's navy and could plan how best to deal with it.

However the agreement confused the British public and international opinion. Only two months earlier, Britain had signed the Stresa Front that had condemned Germany's military build up. Now, Britain was agreeing that Germany could do exactly what Britain had earlier condemned. It also showed Hitler that he could push Britain to revise the Versailles Treaty and get away with it. Were there other parts of Versailles he could challenge?

By the summer of 1935, Hitler was much stronger than he had been at the beginning of the year.

France was scared of German military growth and made a treaty with Russia. Britain was furious. They distrusted communist Russia. Meanwhile, France was angered by Britain's naval deal with Germany.

Britain and France, the allies within the Stresa Front, were now divided, and Italy, the third member of the Stresa Front, was now an enemy of Britain and France.

3 WISE MEN OF STRESA
WENT TO SEA IN A BARREL.

IF THE BARREL HAD BEEN STRONGER
MY STORY WOULD HAVE BEEN LONGER.

The three figures in the floating barrel are Eden (GB) Laval, (France) and Mussolini (Italy). They represent the Stresa front. They are arguing among themselves while around them the periscopes of Hitler's new submarines are watching. Cartoonist Low is commenting on the Stresa Front against Hitler breaking up because of internal arguments and worries about Hitler.

Britain and the Rhineland Crisis

On March 7 1936, Hitler remilitarised the Rhineland. The remilitarisation broke both the Treaty of Versailles and the Treaty of Locarno. The League of Nations had been created partly to maintain the Treaty of Versailles. Clearly Britain and France should have taken action against Hitler.

The Locarno Treaties, signed in 1925 by Germany, France, Italy and Britain, stated that the Rhineland should continue to be demilitarized. Locarno was seen as important because Germany voluntarily accepted the Rhineland as a demilitarized zone.

Why did Britain do nothing about the remilitarisation of the Rhineland?
There are several reasons to explain British lack of action:

- Hitler claimed he was justified.
- Britain was angered by the French alliance with Russia, signed in 1935. The British felt that Hitler had some justification in claiming that remilitarisation was a defensive move to balance the threat on two fronts from Russia and France.
- Public opinion thought Versailles was too harsh. By 1936, many people believed that Germany had been too severely treated at Versailles. As Lord Lothian said, the Germans are 'only moving troops into their own back garden' and Harold Nicolson MP noted in his diary entry for 23 March, 'The feeling in the House of Commons is terribly pro-German.'
- Public opinion did not think the remilitarisation was a serious threat. Remember remilitarisation, was not an invasion or an attack.

There was a very strong anti-war feeling in Britain. Could any politician justify sending British troops to attack Germany, when Germany had attacked no other country? There were no public demonstrations, rallies or protests about remilitarisation anywhere in Britain. The only public demonstrations were 'peace rallies' where the public demanded that the government must not get involved in a war over the crisis. But the government had no intention of using war.

The British government did not see remilitarisation as a problem
The British government was not surprised by remilitarization. Early in 1936, Foreign Secretary Eden had secretly planned for a 'general settlement' that was intended to resolve all of Germany's grievances. Britain was preparing to do a deal with Hitler. In exchange for a German return to the

League of Nations, acceptance of arms limitations, and giving up claims for more land in Europe, Germany would be allowed to remilitarize the Rhineland and would also get back former German African colonies. Britain also wanted talks on an 'air agreement' outlawing bombing.

Had Eden weakened Britain's position?

Yes he had. By offering to discuss remilitarising the Rhineland in exchange for an 'air agreement' Eden signaled to Germany that remilitarization was not considered a vital security threat.

When German troops marched into the Rhineland without an agreement, Britain was left complaining about the way remilitarisation was carried out as opposed to the event itself.

British action would lose more than it gained

Hitler played a smart diplomatic game. The day before remilitarisation took place he made a speech in which he offered most of what Eden had been trying to achieve. Only this time it looked like Hitler was being generous.

With the British government completely against taking action and public opinion against the use of war Britain was never going to take any action against Germany.

Britain also had other concerns that stopped action against Germany

If Hitler was removed from power who – or what – would replace him? The British government feared the spread of Communism across Europe and there was a saying at the time: 'Better Hitlerism than Communism'.

Prime Minister Baldwin claimed that Britain lacked the resources to enforce her treaty guarantees and that public opinion was firmly opposed to any conflict.

The British government also knew they would get no help from the Empire. South Africa and Canada were loudly opposed to becoming involved in any war over the Rhineland.

Could Britain claim the Rhineland crisis was handled successfully?

In the short term, the British government made a virtue out of necessity. They claimed war had been avoided and a grievance from the Peace Settlement had been sorted. But Britain had never been in a position to fight either politically or militarily.

The British government had been caught off-guard by a much smarter Hitler. The remilitarisation of the Rhineland appeared as if Hitler had taken a gamble and the weak democracies had let him get away with it. Once again Hitler had learned a lesson about political manipulation and the willingness of Britain to appease.

In the longer term, the Rhineland crisis sparked off a chain of events that linked Britain to France and Eastern Europe, and eventually the Czech crisis of 1938.

How did Britain become involved in East European tensions?

Britain had no commitments in Eastern Europe but the answer lies with a statement made in March 1936 by the British government.

France was worried by the remilitarisation of the Rhineland and wanted to take some action. Britain persuaded France not to act but held talks about combined action in the future. After the meeting, Britain issued a statement intended to reassure France. The statement on 19 March 1936 said that Britain considered French security to be a vital national need. In the future it was clear that any French involvement in Eastern Europe would almost inevitably involve Britain.

Why was France involved in Eastern Europe?

France had spent almost its entire military budget on the Maginot Line, a huge line of fortifications, much of it underground. The French felt safe behind their Maginot line, described by one observer as 'an expensive hidey-hole'. French military planning was defensive, summed up as 'the Maginot Mentality'.

On the other hand, France had made alliances with eastern European countries in the 1920s in an attempt to surround Germany. Now, in the 1930s, any threat to Eastern Europe would involve France. But should that concern Britain?

In this way, the British government found itself drawn into the Central European crisis of 1938. The French–Czechoslovak alliance of 1924 meant any German–Czechoslovak war would automatically become a French–German war and because of the statement of 19 March 1936 there would be strong pressure on Britain to help France.

Was British policy a success?

No. War was never a possibility over the Rhineland so Britain had to accept the inevitable. Hitler did not carry through any of the offers he made at the time of remilitarisation. Eden's plan for a negotiation with Germany never happened.

France was resentful of British inaction and fearful of Germany.

The remilitarisation of the Rhineland effectively 'locked the door' on the western frontier of Germany. Hitler started to build a line of fortifications along the German–French border called the 'Siegfried line'. He then turned his attention to eastern European expansion and Lebensraum – with huge consequences for France and Britain.

Britain and the Spanish Civil War

The Spanish Civil War lasted from 1936 to 1939. Supporters of the legal, legitimate government of Spain were called Republicans. The supporters of rebels, led by General Franco, were called Nationalists.

The war started because of tensions in Spain but the international importance of the civil war lies in how it was affected by the actions, or lack of action, of the major European powers. In the end the Nationalists won. A major reason was the help they received from Germany and Italy while the Republicans got very little outside help.

Non-intervention

Britain was determined not to let the Spanish Civil War grow into a big European war. The official policy of Britain was non-intervention. Foreign Secretary Anthony Eden described British policy as follows:

> 'The policy of non-intervention has limited and bit-by-bit reduced the flow of foreign intervention in arms and men into Spain. Even more important, the policy has greatly reduced the risk of a general war'.

When the war began, the French government intended to send help to the Republicans. The British then persuaded the French to push for non-intervention. British and French leaders, Baldwin and Blum, called for all countries in Europe not to intervene in the Spanish Civil War. The first meeting of the Non-Intervention Committee met in London on 9 September 1936. Eventually 27 countries including Germany, Britain, France, the Soviet Union, Portugal, Sweden and Italy signed the Non-Intervention Agreement.

The official British policy can be seen as another step in the development of appeasement

Neither Britain nor France, who had organised the Non-Intervention Committee, stood up against the interventionist policies of the dictators.

Vital member states of the Non-Intervention Committee such as Germany and Italy broke their promises and sent help to the Nationalist side. The German ambassador to Britain in 1937, von Ribbentrop, said, 'A better name for the Non-Intervention Committee would have been the Intervention Committee.'

Why did the British government want intervention?

There are four main questions that may help explain Britain's position.

1. Did Britain adopt the policy of non-intervention because the Government was afraid of Nazi and Fascist power?
2. Did Britain feel that it could not take action because more time was needed to rearm?
3. Did the British government sympathise politically with the aims and values of the rebel Nationalists?
4. Was Britain afraid that a Republican victory would lead to a Communist controlled Spain, something Britain feared?

Was non-intervention popular with the British public?

Some people were very much against the policy. These people tended to be socialist or communist and many were members of the Labour Party. Rallies were held in support of the Republicans and collections were taken to raise money. However, writer and member of the International Brigade,

Appeasement and the road to war

George Orwell, wrote that more money was spent by the British public on the football pools (a sort of football-based lottery) in one week, than was raised to help Spain over three years.

The majority were scared of war and happy if it did not affect them. However, some young British men and women did feel strongly enough to go to Spain to fight against Fascism. They joined the International Brigades.

What were the International Brigades?

The International Brigades were made up of ordinary people who gave up their jobs and travelled to Spain so that they could make a personal stand against what they saw as the growth of Fascism in Europe. As Jack Jones of the British Labour Party said:

> 'We believe that there can be no compromise between Fascism and Democratic ideals, for which we ourselves have come here to fight.'

The volunteers were not regular soldiers but were often disillusioned by the weak appeasement policies of their own democratic governments. They were mainly communist volunteers from many different countries including France, Britain, Canada and the USA. In total there were about 50 000 men and women from 53 countries. There were even Italian and German Communists in the International Brigades who fought Fascist Italian and German troops. The Spanish Civil War is sometimes called 'Europe's Civil War'.

The Brigades fought with courage but their inexperience led to high casualty rates. Many were disillusioned when they found themselves being used by Communist authorities to fight against other Republican groups such as the Socialists and the Anarchists. The Brigades were withdrawn from Spain in October 1938 as the position of the republic became desperate.

Could British policy be called a success?

In one way, non-intervention could be called a success because a major European war was not sparked off by the Spanish war.

On the other hand, Britain faced many difficulties because of its non-intervention policy.

The Republican government of Spain was the democratically elected government. It had the right to buy weapons on the international market with which to defend itself. Britain urged that arms should not be sent to either side. That way the rebels were being treated the same as the elected government. That was legally wrong. Britain was discredited as a defender of democracy.

The ban on arms sales did not hurt the rebels as they got supplies from the fascist powers.

Britain argued the war was a civil war they should keep out of. However the League of Nations should have taken steps to help the Republic. Britain made sure it did not.

The British government also had to face very loud criticism at home from the Labour Party who strongly disagreed with the policy and from individuals who went to join the International Brigades.

Internationally, Britain and France seemed to be paralysed. Both countries appeared to lack the resolve or the resources to offer support to the legitimate Spanish government. The confidence of Germany and Italy was boosted.

The USSR now suspected that they could expect no help from Britain and France if the Nazis attacked Russia. Later, the Munich meeting of 1938 confirmed the feelings of the USSR and led down a direct path of self-interest to the Nazi–Soviet Agreement of August 1939 and thereby directly to World War Two. You'll see how that happened later in the last section.

Although Britain took no direct part in the war, the British public felt the effects of the war. Newsreels showing the bombing of Madrid and Guernica, a Spanish town, by German aircraft, code named 'the Condor Legion', came to symbolise the fear that in a future war bombing of cities would cause massive loss of life.

Selfishly, most of the British public were quite happy that wars could be fought elsewhere and not involve Britain.

Britain and the Anschluss crisis, March 1938

In March 1938, German troops marched into Austria, against the rules of the Treaty of Versailles. Britain and France appeased Hitler and did nothing to help Austria.

Was Britain surprised by Anschluss?

No. Hitler had shown his intention to take over Austria as early as 1934. At that time Mussolini blocked Hitler. By 1936, Germany and Austria had grown closer with an agreement to cooperate more closely on many issues.

In February 1938, Hitler tried to put pressure on Schuschnigg, the Austrian Chancellor. At a meeting in February 1938, Hitler told Schuschnigg that Austria could expect no help from Britain and France and that Germany was now allied to Italy, the former protector of Austria.

Schuschnigg was scared and returned to Austria hoping to drum up international support. He planned a plebiscite (also called a referendum) to ask the Austrian people if they wanted to be German or if they wanted to stay Austrian. Schuschnigg was gambling that if the Austrians voted to stay separate from Germany the whole world would know that Hitler had no excuse to invade Austria. The plebiscite was planned for March 13 but Hitler ordered Schuschnigg to call it off.

Meanwhile, Chamberlain, the British Prime Minister, had said, 'Why should we mislead... [small European countries]... by giving them an assurance of security when any such security can only be a delusion? '

Faced by the reality that he could expect no help from Britain or France, Schuschnigg resigned. On 12 March 1938, German troops marched unopposed into Austria. Britain was concerned but not surprised.

The reaction of Britain and France to Anschluss.

The terms of the Versailles agreement were perfectly clear – Anschluss was forbidden. However, once again Britain and France did nothing and therefore Austria takes its place in the story of appeasement.

On 7 March 1938 Neville Chamberlain said:

> 'What small country in Europe today, if threatened by a larger one, can safely rely on the League alone to protect it from invasion?... There can only be one honest answer to it, and that is ''none''.'

In the very first sentence, Chamberlain made it clear there was no longer any faith in collective security and that, apart from appeasement, there was nothing much more that could be done.

Opinion in Britain was divided about what to do. Most people in Britain believed that Austria was not a British problem and it was too far away to give any help. You already know that many British people felt that Versailles had been too harsh and as Austria shared a common culture and language with Germany, Anschluss was inevitable.

On the other hand, anti-appeasers felt that Hitler was a bully who would keep coming back for more unless he was stopped and that appeasement just encouraged Hitler's aggression.

More practically, politicians such as Winston Churchill felt that Anschluss gained Hitler resources, factories and men of military age and control over south Eastern Europe.

In a speech in the House of Commons in March 1938 Churchill said:

> 'We cannot leave the Austrian question where it is. The public mind has been concentrated upon the Nazi conquest of Austria – a small country brutally struck down. Vienna is the centre of all the countries lying to the south east of Europe. A long stretch of the River Danube is now in German hands. The mastery of Vienna gives to Nazi Germany military and economic control of the whole of the communications of South East Europe by road, river and rail. What's the effect of this upon what is called the balance of power?'

But remember, although Churchill consistently opposed appeasement, he was not Prime minister at the time of Anschluss. He was very much a 'voice in the wilderness '.

Majority opinion sided with the views of Lord Tweedsmuir, who said:

> 'I do not myself quite see what there is to fuss about. Austria will be much more comfortable, economically under Germany's wing. That should have been done long ago in the Versailles Treaty. Surely the Versailles agreement was the most half-witted thing ever carried out.'

In terms of resisting Fascist aggression and preparing for the future, appeasement over Anschluss weakened Britain's position.

Britain had for a long time been aware of Hitler's ambitions in Eastern Europe – Lebensraum. In November 1937, Hitler had called his generals to a meeting. Only one note of the discussions survived. A young officer called Hossbach wrote it. The Hossbach memorandum is an important piece of evidence to show that Hitler was planning a war. The Hossbach memorandum made clear that Hitler planned to take Austria and Czechoslovakia at the same time, possibly in 1938. They were the first stage in his move eastwards towards Russia.

The Schushnigg plebiscite had forced Hitler to move faster than he intended but once Austria was taken over by Nazi Germany it was clear to see where Hitler's next move would be. The western part of Czechoslovakia had German troops to its north, west and south. It would be easy for German forces to move in. Czechoslovakia was like old-fashioned circus entertainers whose act was to place their heads into a lion's open mouth. The trick was to stop the lion snapping his jaws shut on the head. Czechoslovakia was to have no such luck.

Although Britain could do little to stop Anschluss, the policy of appeasement was making it very easy for Hitler to move eastwards and seize more land in his move towards Lebensraum. Those moves would involve France because of alliances France had with Czechoslovakia and Poland. Britain would then become involved because of the statement Britain had made about France in March 1936.

Finally, as a result of British inaction, no small European country had any belief that Britain or France could or would really help them. Appeasement was seen as a policy to benefit Britain only and help no one else.

Practise your skills

This section shows you how to plan an essay based on the question:

How successfully did British foreign policy manage to contain fascist aggression between 1935 and March 1938?

Remember – topic and task!

Decide what the question is about (the topic) – this essay is about aggressive moves made by Germany and Italy and what Britain did in response to those things. You should recognise that British Foreign policy between 1935 and 1938 is another way of asking about appeasement.

Decide what you have to do (the task) – judge how successfully Britain dealt with the problems. Beware! To answer this question well you must know what the aims of appeasement were. If you don't make that clear how else can you judge if the policy was a success?

You must also be clear what events can be included as 'fascist aggression.' Relevant events include:

- the Abyssinian crisis
- rearmament and the Naval Treaty
- the Rhineland remilitarisation
- Fascist intervention in the Spanish Civil War
- Anschluss

Essay advice
Introduction
Here is a good introduction that you use as a base to develop a full answer; it builds on tips on essay writing that you should have picked up in the earlier examples in this book:

Between 1935 and March 1938, British foreign policy was called 'appeasement'. The aim of appeasement was partly to resolve grievances often resulting from the treaties at the end of the Great War and also to avoid a major European war that would involve Britain.

Beginning in 1935, Britain appeased Mussolini over Abyssinia (1) and Hitler over rearmament (2). In 1936, Britain responded to the Rhineland Crisis (3) and the outbreak of the Spanish Civil War (4). Finally, in March 1938 Britain was faced with Anschluss and the beginning of Hitler's move towards Eastern Europe (5).

The middle
Your introduction has outlined the criteria for success (resolve grievances and avoid war) and also the main examples of Fascist aggression.

Each numbered section should be developed in one paragraph containing relevant accurate information about the event, British reaction and whether or not you think their action was successful.

In judging success you will probably find there are two different points of view. For example, when dealing with the naval treaty in 1935 the British government said it accepted the inevitable and at least gave Britain an idea how many ships Germany would build. On the other hand, not only did it encourage Hitler to think the Treaty of Versailles could be easily broken in other ways but it assumed Hitler would keep his promises and we know in hindsight that he did not!

How was appeasement (or non-intervention in Spain) applied? Was it successful using the criteria established at the beginning – did Britain prevent a major European War?

Your conclusion
Follow the advice about conclusions given at the end of Issue 1. Here is an example of a reasonably good conclusion that sums up an argument and links directly to the question.

In conclusion, British foreign policy in the shape of appeasement seemed to be successful.

On one hand, no large European war started and Britain was not dragged into any conflict.

On the other hand, the rules of the League were ignored, the Treaty of Versailles almost abandoned, democratically elected governments were attacked and overthrown without any intervention from Britain, and smaller states were allowed to be taken over by Nazi expansion.

Overall, while Britain avoided war, Fascist states were encouraged and perhaps the best thing that can be said for British foreign policy up to March 1938 is that it delayed war rather than preventing it altogether.

Issue 5 – The Munich agreement – good or bad?

The big picture

By the summer of 1938, another international crisis was brewing – this time over Czechoslovakia. The heart of the crisis was the Sudetenland, a part of Czechoslovakia. The crisis seemed to be solved by an agreement at Munich. The Munich agreement is still controversial. Some historians believe the agreement was a practical solution given the circumstances of the time. Others believe Munich was a cowardly sell-out of an ally.

The background to the crisis

Czechoslovakia was a new country created after the Great War. It contained many different nationalities of which there were 3 million German speakers who lived in an area called the Sudetenland. In 1938, Europe was close to war because of a crisis over the Sudetenland. Hitler claimed the German speaking population of the Sudetenland was being persecuted. This was his excuse to justify taking the territory over. Don't make the mistake of thinking Hitler wanted the Sudetenland back. It had never been part of Germany. The land had been part of the Austrian–Hungarian Empire until 1919. However the population did speak German so they were fair game for Hitler!

Why did Hitler really want Czechoslovakia?

Hitler's ambition of Lebensraum meant eastwards expansion towards Russia, but Czechoslovakia, with its strong defences, was a barrier to his plans. If Hitler got the frontier area of the Sudetenland, it would be easy to make further advances into Czechoslovakia.

Czechoslovakia was in a very vulnerable position. After Anschluss, Nazi-controlled territory bordered western Czechoslovakia to the north, the west and the south.

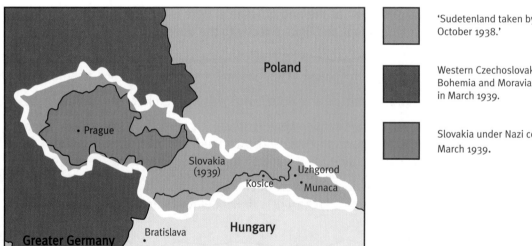

'Sudetenland taken by Hitler In October 1938.'

Western Czechoslovakia called Bohemia and Moravia taken by Hitler in March 1939.

Slovakia under Nazi control from March 1939.

Appeasement and the road to war

How did Hitler destabilise the Sudetenland?

Hitler encouraged the growth of a Sudeten German party, led by Konrad Henlein, to provoke trouble in the Sudetenland. By August 1938, Hitler was making wild, nationalistic speeches that encouraged pro-Nazi demonstrations in the Sudetenland. Hitler hoped that those demonstrations would cause the Czech police to take strong action against the Sudeten protestors. Hitler would then have his excuse to invade claiming he was protecting the Sudeten Germans from Czech persecution.

Why was Britain worried?

Back in May 1938, Hitler had secretly ordered his army to be ready to attack Czechoslovakia by 1 October. Britain knew about the plan. That deadline provides the reason why there was such desperate activity in September 1938. Chamberlain was well aware of the risk that Britain would be dragged into a war.

Why was Britain involved in the Czech crisis?

Czechoslovakia would fight if attacked by Germany. France had an alliance with Czechoslovakia and might therefore fight to help its ally. Britain had no intention of being sucked into a war because of France's alliance with Czechoslovakia, and France had no intention of going to war without British support. However, Britain could not sit back and watch a war erupt just across the English Channel. In a statement in March 1936, Britain had described French security as a vital British interest. Britain would inevitably become involved. Britain and France had to find a way to get 'off the hook'.

Why did Chamberlain get involved?

The British Prime Minister, Neville Chamberlain, was determined to avoid a war. He was determined to make appeasement work and flew three times to meet Hitler during September 1938. Air journeys were risky and uncomfortable at that time. Add the fact that Chamberlain was an old man and you get the idea that September 1938 really was crunch time for Britain, appeasement and the chances of peace.

On 12 September the Czech crisis got worse. Hitler made a speech that hinted heavily that Germany would help the Sudeten Germans gain their independence from Czechoslovakia. Hitler expected Henlein to lead protests against the Czech government. The Czech government would probably take strong action and then Hitler would have his excuse to intervene. War was looking dangerously close.

In the space of two weeks, between 15 and 29 September, Chamberlain flew three times to meet with Hitler.

Meeting one: Berchtesgaden, 15 September 1938
On 15 September, Chamberlain made the first of three visits in two weeks to Hitler.

Hitler demanded the Sudetenland at some point in the future. Chamberlain returned to Britain and gained the agreement of France and Czechoslovakia. Chamberlain was pleased because he seemed to have solved the crisis.

France was relieved because they could now claim they had done their best to secure Czechoslovakia's future.

Czechoslovakia was left feeling bitter because their ally France had abandoned them and they were forced to agree to hand over their territory.

Meeting two: Bad Godesberg, 22 September 1938
A week after the first meeting with Hitler, Chamberlain went into the second meeting confident that the Sudeten problem had been solved. But Hitler had other plans. He was determined to provoke a war and said he wanted the Sudetenland immediately or there would be war. Chamberlain was horrified by Hitler's change of demands. He returned to Britain expecting war to break out and made a BBC broadcast to the British public:

> 'How horrible and unbelievable it is that we should be getting ready for war, trying on gas masks and digging air raid shelters in Britain because of a far away quarrel between people that we know nothing about.'

War was likely. Hitler had demanded a reply from Britain by 2 pm on 28 September. The offer of a new meeting – in Munich – came just before 2pm.

Meeting three: Munich, 29 September 1938
At the Munich Conference, Britain, France, Germany and Italy (Germany's ally) met to discuss the future of the Sudetenland.

It was agreed that Germany was to get the Sudetenland almost immediately. Czechoslovakia's leaders were not invited to the Conference and their territory was given away without their agreement.

At a private meeting between Hitler and Chamberlain, Hitler promised he had no more territorial demands to make in Europe and that there would be no war between Britain and Germany.

The Munich Agreement – realism or sell out?

The Munich settlement is central to any study of appeasement in the 1930s. The carve-up of Czechoslovakia without Czech representatives being part of the agreement seemed the ultimate betrayal of a friend.

Churchill described the Munich settlement as 'an unmitigated defeat'.

A typical anti-Munich point of view was expressed in a letter written at the time:

> 'I am sure that when the world hears of the Munich agreement thousands of people ... will be shocked and humiliated. Hitler has got everything he wanted without firing a shot. Britain has thrown Czechoslovakia to the wolves.' *The Kilmarnock Review*, October 1938

However, there are others who argue that Chamberlain had little choice and Munich prevented the war that seemed likely to start in October 1938. Undoubtedly, Chamberlain manipulated the media to put a positive 'spin' on the Munich agreement but it is true to say that most of the public would rather 'sell Czechoslovakia down the river', as one commentator put it, than risk war with Germany.

Hitler was given the Sudetenland as the price of avoiding war. As Hitler said, 'I have no more territorial demands to make in Europe,' and Chamberlain's private talk with Hitler at Munich resulted in the famous 'piece of paper' that promised 'peace in our time'.

Although it is hard to see Munich as 'Peace with honour', as Chamberlain claimed, perhaps it can be seen as a realistic response to the situation at the time. As historian, A.J.P. Taylor, pointed out in the 1960s:

> 'The settlement at Munich was a triumph for British policy, not for Hitler. Hitler had wanted to take land by force. Britain had wanted to avoid conflict. Appeasement had not been created as a policy to save Austria or Czechoslovakia. It was created to keep peace and avoid war by negotiation. With that definition how can people criticise Chamberlain at Munich? '

In Britain, most people were greatly relieved that war had been avoided. Few looked to the future implications of such a settlement. The fear of war, especially gas bombing, was enough to make the public glad that peace had been purchased, even temporarily, at some other country's cost.

A cartoon at the time showed Chamberlain outside the 'World Theatre' promising *Catastrophe* as its next production. Chamberlain is shown sticking a new poster across *Catastrophe*. The new poster simply says, 'Postponed'. Most of the British population hoped for peace but realised the Munich settlement had only just delayed the inevitable.

Events in March 1939 were to prove their suspicions correct.

Practise your skills

This section shows you how to plan an essay based on the question:

To what extent can the Munich agreement be considered a success for British policy?

Remember – topic and task!

This essay topic is the Munich agreement of September 1938.

You need to do three main things:

1. Show off your knowledge about the Munich agreement
2. State what arguments support the idea that it was a success for Britain
3. State what arguments support the idea that it was not a success for Britain.

Your task is to come to a balanced conclusion about the agreement. You do not have to make a strong decision yourself but if you do have a point of view you must support it with the evidence in your essay.

You must also be clear about what events can be included in the story of the Munich Agreement. You must show detailed knowledge of the following:

- Hitler's ambitions for Lebensraum
- how Anschluss made Czechoslovakia more vulnerable
- the Sudeten Crisis of September 1938
- why the Sudeten Crisis could involve France and Britain in a war
- Chamberlain's three flights
- the Munich Agreement
- contrasting views on the agreement

Essay advice

Introduction

Here is a good introduction that you can use as a base to develop a full answer. It builds on tips on essay writing you should have picked up in the earlier examples in this book.

> The Sudeten crisis had threatened to lead to a war (1) that Britain and France were desperate to avoid (2). Chamberlain had three meetings with Hitler (3). At Munich a settlement was reached that seemed to end the crisis (4). When Chamberlain returned to Britain, crowds cheered their hero (5). On the other hand, many people felt Czechoslovakia had been betrayed (6). Why did the Munich agreement lead to such different points of view (7)?

The middle

Your introduction has raised seven possible development points. The bulk of your essay should now use accurate and relevant information to expand on those development points. To help you, each numbered point has a core question that must be dealt with. The last point has several ideas to help you.

1. What was the Sudeten crisis all about?
2. Why could France and Britain become involved in a war over a crisis in Czechoslovakia?
3. How did the three meetings with Hitler show the escalation of the Czech crisis?
4. What was agreed at the Munich conference and in the private meeting between Chamberlain and Hitler?
5. For what reasons can the Munich agreement be seen as a success for British policy?
6. Why did people criticise the Munich agreement?
7. This is the main question in the essay. Did the Munich agreement help buy time for Britain? Did it sell out an ally? Did Britain have any responsibility to Czechoslovakia? Were the cheering crowds manipulated by the media at the time to support Chamberlain? Why was Russia made angry by the agreement and did that lead to later problems in reaching agreements with Russia? Was appeasement not meant to negotiate away grievances – and did not the Munich agreement do that? Or did it just encourage Hitler to make his next step eastwards that eventually led to war?

Your conclusion

Having gone through those points you will have analysed the Munich Agreement.

By reading back over advice on essay writing given earlier in this book it is now up to you to write an appropriate conclusion.

Use the four-phase model outlined earlier starting with, 'In conclusion'. Good luck!

Issue 6 – Was the end of appeasement the reason for war breaking out in 1939?

> ## The big picture
> When Hitler spread Nazi control over the rest of Czechoslovakia in March 1939 appeasement was discredited. Both Britain and France promised to support Poland and Romania if Hitler attacked them. But why should those promises mean any more than other that had been broken? Throughout the summer of 1939 Hitler increased pressure on Poland, especially in the Polish Corridor. Britain hoped that Russia might be persuaded to help defend Poland but when Nazi Germany reached an agreement with Communist Russia in August 1939 Poland was doomed. Would Britain and France keep their promise to help Poland?

Why was the policy of appeasement abandoned?

At the Munich meeting Hitler had said, 'Europe can look forward to a Christmas of Peace.' In fact, Hitler's promise that he had 'no more territorial demands in Europe' only lasted six months.

In March 1939 Hitler tore up the promises made at Munich and invaded the western part of Czechoslovakia called Bohemia and Moravia. The eastern half of Czechoslovakia became the Slovak State but under Nazi control.

By moving into Czechoslovakia and Austria, Hitler had created a geographical problem for Britain. Where would he go next? Hitler had two different ways he could attack Russia – one north-eastwards through Poland, the other south-eastwards through Romania.

Hitler's actions effectively destroyed any hopes that appeasement might prevent war. Public opinion in Britain and France moved towards an acceptance that Hitler could only be stopped by force.

On 1 April 1939 Chamberlain announced:

> 'In the event of any action which clearly threatened Polish independence and which the Polish Government accordingly considered it vital to resist with their national forces, the Government would feel themselves bound at once to lend the Polish help. I may add that the French Government have authorised me to make it plain that they stand in the same position in this matter as do his Majesty's Government.'

A few weeks later the British government began to prepare an army to fight in Europe.

How did Hitler react to Britain's change of policy?

Within two days of Chamberlain's speech, Hitler had ordered his army to plan for an attack on Poland on or just after the beginning of September. By the end of April, Hitler announced that he would no longer be limited by promises he made to Poland in the 1934 non-aggression pact.

Hitler only expected a short war with Poland. After all, given Britain's failure to take action to stop Hitler on many previous occasions, why should Hitler worry now?

How did Hitler create a Polish crisis?

By the summer of 1939 it was clear Hitler was aiming to take Poland. Once again Hitler used his tried and tested methods of building up tension and creating excuses for Germany to take action against Poland.

Poland was created at the end of the Great War, partly from land taken from Germany and Russia. Check on a map of the time to see how land given to Poland called the 'Polish Corridor' divided the bulk of Germany from a smaller part called East Prussia.

The Polish Corridor contained mostly German-speaking people. It also contained the important port of Danzig and Hitler wanted it back under his control. Naturally, Hitler complained about the treatment of Germans in the Polish Corridor. The Polish Corridor issue became Hitler's excuse for pressurising Poland in 1939.

Why was Russia important to the Polish crisis?

Britain hoped that an alliance with Russia would make Hitler stop his moves against Poland. Any attack on Poland would take Germany up to the border with Russia and Britain guessed Hitler would not risk a war with Russia. But would Russia be prepared to fight for Poland?

The leader of Russia, Joseph Stalin, was worried that Russia would be invaded by Germany. Russia was not ready to fight and Stalin knew that he needed either strong allies or more time to build up Russian defences. Stalin was also annoyed and suspicious of Britain and France. He had not been invited to the Munich conference and in April 1939 Russia's suggestion of an alliance with Britain was rejected. Stalin was convinced that Britain was encouraging Hitler to move eastwards against Russia. That way Britain could watch Hitlerism and Communism destroy one another.

Why did Britain and Russia not make an alliance against Hitler?

Winston Churchill realised the vital importance of an alliance with Russia when he said:

> 'There is no means of maintaining an eastern front against Nazi aggression without the active aid of Russia.'

However, by the summer of 1939, no deal between Poland, Britain and Russia had been made.

The real reason for lack of diplomatic progress was that Britain was reluctant to make an agreement with communist Russia. Chamberlain, the British prime minister, was not keen to form an alliance with the Soviet Union and wrote, 'I must confess to the most profound distrust of Russia. I distrust her motives, which seem to me to have little connection with our ideas of liberty. ' Another difficulty in creating an alliance between Britain and Russia was Poland's attitude. Poland was an old enemy of Russia and under no circumstances would allow Russian soldiers into Poland – even to fight a common enemy.

The negotiations proceeded slowly throughout the summer of 1939. Britain felt there was no rush. Given the hatred between Russia and Germany, Britain felt they could take as long as they wanted before tying themselves to an alliance with Communist Russia, also known as the Soviet Union.

By August little had happened. Stalin knew he had to do something to buy time. The only way he could do that was to make a deal with Hitler!

The Nazi–Soviet Non-Aggression Agreement

The agreement signed between Hitler and Stalin on August 23, 1939 shocked the world because each side was supposed to be the sworn enemy of the other. It was called the Nazi–Soviet Non-Aggression Pact, or sometimes the Molotov–Ribbentrop agreement after the Russian and German negotiators.

The agreement stated that Germany and Russia would not fight each other. There was also a secret part to the agreement. In private, Stalin and Hitler had agreed to divide up Poland between them!

The immediate consequence of the agreement was that Stalin had bought time, Hitler could have a short limited war with Poland – and Poland was doomed.

How did Hitler push a crisis into war?

In August 1939, Hitler claimed a German radio tower had been attacked. He claimed the attackers had all been killed. Hitler showed the dead Polish soldiers lying on German territory. In reality Hitler had ordered some prisoners to be dressed in Polish army uniforms and then shot. The bodies were dumped near the radio tower. Hitler had his excuse. He claimed that Poland was attempting to invade Germany and one week after the Nazi–Soviet agreement was signed, Nazi tanks rolled into Poland on 1 September 1939.

A short, sharp war?

When Hitler invaded Poland he believed he would have a short, easy war. Russia was now on his side and although Britain and France had promised to fight for Poland, there was no way they could send help across Europe. Hitler was sure that Britain would back down and France would follow Britain's lead. They had always given in before but this time there was no appeasement. As Anthony Eden, the former foreign secretary said in a radio broadcast on 29 August 1939:

> 'Our obligations to Poland will of course be honoured. The world has to choose between order and anarchy. For too long it has staggered from crisis to crisis under the constant threat of armed force. We cannot live forever at the pistol point. The love of the British people for peace is as great as ever, but they are no less determined that this time peace shall be based on the denial of force and a respect for the pledged word.'

When Nazi troops invaded Poland on 1 September, Chamberlain warned Hitler to retreat by 11am on Sunday 3 September or face the consequences. On the morning of 3 September 1939, Chamberlain spoke on radio to the British people to tell them that, 'This country is at war with Germany,' because the German invasion of Poland was continuing. Britain's declaration of war on Germany was followed by similar declarations from Australia, New Zealand, France, South Africa and Canada. World War Two had started. Appeasement was dead.

Practise your skills

This section shows you how to plan an essay based on the question:

To what extent was the ending of appeasement responsible for war breaking out in September 1939?

Essay advice

By using all the advice you have been given on eay writing it is now time to create your own essay from scratch.

You know you need a signposted introduction, several well-developed paragraphs with relevant accurate detail and finally you need a strong four-phase conclusion.

Good luck!

Napoleon Bonaparte

b. August 15, 1759, d. May 5, 1821

Napoleon rose to fame during the French Revolution (1789–1799). As commander of the French Revolutionary armies he seized political power and proclaimed himself Emperor of France in 1804. His military victories extended French rule over much of Europe. Although Napoleon was seen as a terrible threat by the old aristocratic rulers of Europe, the Liberals and Nationalists at first saw him as the person who could bring about change. After all, the slogan of the French Revolution was Liberté, Egalité, Fraternité (Liberty, Equality, Fraternity).

However, it soon became clear that Napoleon was not going to free Europe; but rather, he enslaved it by strictly controlling his conquered territories. In 1815, Napoleon's ambitions were finally crushed by defeat at the Battle of Waterloo at the hands of British, Dutch and Prussian soldiers, led by the Duke of Wellington. About one million French soldiers had died in battle or as a result of disease during the 11 years of the Napoleonic Wars. In hindsight, Napoleon upset the European political balance of power. The ideals of the French Revolution were at the root of most of Europe's political changes in the 19th century but, when Napoleon died in 1821, it looked as if the Old Order was back in control.

Prince Klemens von Metternich

b. May 15, 1773, d. June 11, 1859

Metterich was born in Koblenz in the Rhineland. Between 1809 and 1848, he was Foreign Minister of the Austrian Empire and Chancellor between 1821 and 1848. He believed that strong government was needed to prevent revolution. He was opposed to Nationalism and Liberalism, ideologies which he believed threatened the Austrian Empire. He also tried to maintain the power of Austria at the expense of Prussia.

Metternich helped defeat Napoleon, for which he was made a prince in 1813. He was a major influence in creating the German Confederation under an Austrian presidency in 1815. Metternich became a symbol of the Old Order which stood against change. He was forced from power by the Revolutions of 1848, after which he fled to Britain. Just before he died, he said, 'I was a rock of order'.

Otto von Bismarck

b. April 1, 1815, d. July 30, 1898

Bismarck's family were landowners in Prussia and in the Revolutions of 1848, Bismarck made it clear he was against change and even supported the continued Austrian leadership in Germany. In the 1850s, he was Prussian Minister to the German Confederation in Frankfurt and worked to secure Prussian interests, without regard to consistent policy or ideology. After a short time representing Prussia in St. Petersburg and Paris, he was asked to become Minister-President and Foreign Minister for the Prussian King, Wilhelm I.

Bismarck is remembered as the man who brought about German unification between 1864 and 1871, mainly as a result of three wars against Denmark, Austria and France. These wars demonstrated Bismarck's diplomacy, his ability to plan and also his ability to make use of chance occurrences and manipulate events to his advantage.

His diplomacy brought victorious wars against Denmark (over Schleswig-Holstein in 1864) and against Austria (the Seven Weeks War of 1866). The North German Confederation was formed in 1867 under Prussian control. In 1870, Bismarck's backing of a Hohenzollern prince as candidate for the Spanish throne led to war against France. After France was defeated, the German Empire was proclaimed at Versailles on January 18, 1871, and Bismarck became German Chancellor.

As Chancellor, Bismarck's foreign policy was directed at maintaining and strengthening the power of the German Empire. To that end, he established a network of alliances called the Bismarck system, his main concern being to isolate France so that she would never achieve her dream of revenge against Germany.

Domestically, Bismarck was concerned with maintaining Prussian authority over the newly united Germany. The new constitution, although seemingly democratic, merely disguised the power held by Bismarck through his influence over the Kaiser. Bismarck was also concerned with keeping Germany safe from internal threats to its unity. In the 1870s, Bismarck considered Catholics to be a threat and spent many years trying to undermine Catholic influence in Germany. However, when Bismarck found Socialism to be a bigger threat he abandoned his anti-Catholic policies (the Kulturkampf) and began a series of policies aimed at weakening the attraction of Socialism. In 1890, the new Kaiser disagreed with Bismarck over his policies towards the Socialists and so Bismarck resigned.

In the short term, Bismarck's policies kept his new, young creation – Germany – stable, but in the longer term he kept alive the power of the landed aristocracy in Germany and, under Wilhelm II, Bismarck's alliance system contributed directly to World War I and the collapse of the German Empire.

Paul von Hindenburg

b. October 2, 1847, d. August 2, 1934

Hindenburg served as a German field marshal in World War I. In the mid 1920s, the new democratic Weimar Republic had few strong supporters. Most people were disillusioned with democratic party politics and the problems facing Germany as a result of losing World War I. Some historians explain Hindenburg's victory in the Presidential election of 1925 by claiming that, for many Germans, Hindenburg represented stability, a living reminder of the good old days of pre-war Germany and even a substitute Kaiser. Hindenburg was re-elected as President in 1932 but by this time he was an old man, easily under the influence of politicians who hoped to use his presidential powers for their own ends.

Hindenburg hated Hitler, but was persuaded to appoint him Chancellor. Following Hindenburg's death in 1934, democracy in Germany was all but dead as Hitler established his dictatorship.

Arthur Neville Chamberlain

b. March 18, 1869, d. November 9, 1940

Between 1931 and 1937, Chamberlain served in the British National Government as Chancellor of the Exchequer. As Prime Minister from 1937 to 1940, he will always be linked to the policy of Appeasement. Critics of Chamberlain argue that his failure to stand up against Nazi aggression encouraged Hitler to make even more demands; whilst his supporters believe that appeasement was a sensible policy at the time, given Britain's relative weakness and public opinion which was strongly anti-war until 1939. During the Czechoslovakian crisis of 1938, Chamberlain met Hitler several times and he returned from the Munich Conference claiming to have secured 'peace for our time.' Although Chamberlain was cheered as a hero in October 1938, he was discredited when Hitler broke his promises the following year. He resigned as Prime Minister in 1940 and died a few weeks later.

Benito Mussolini

b. July 29, 1883, d. April 28, 1945

Founder of Italian Fascism and Premier (1922–43) of Italy, Mussolini ruled Italy as dictator from 1925. In 1912, Mussolini was the editor of the Socialist Party newspaper Avanti! and when World War I began in 1914 was opposed to Italy's involvement. However, he changed his mind and was expelled from the Socialist Party. He served in the army until he was wounded in 1917. In 1919, Mussolini and others founded the Fasci di Combattimento, a new nationalist party, in Milan. This Fascist movement was against Socialists, Communists and Democrats. By 1925–26, he had created a single-party, totalitarian dictatorship. Mussolini was known as Il Duce ('the leader').

In the mid 1930s, Mussolini adopted an aggressive foreign policy, conquering Abyssinia in 1936 and helping General Franco win the Spanish Civil War. Also in 1936, Mussolini and Hitler became allies, a friendship which led to the Rome-Berlin Axis and which fundamentally altered the balance of power in Europe in favour of these two dictators. Mussolini passed laws which discriminated against Italy's Jews and did nothing to stop German troops who captured these people from their homes and took them to concentration camps in Germany. Once Britain realised Mussolini could not be relied on as an ally against Hitler, it was almost inevitable that the policy of appeasement would continue. Italy joined World War Two against Britain in 1940, but, by 1943, had lost all support in Italy and was imprisoned. However, he was freed by a daring German rescue only two months later and was made head of a Fascist puppet government in North Italy. In 1945, while trying to escape advancing allied armies, Mussolini and his mistress were captured by Italian partisans who shot them both. Their bodies were brought to Milan and hung upside down in a public square before being buried in an unmarked grave.

Although Mussolini had been popular with most Italians until the late 1930s, he lost their support when he took them into an unpopular war which Italy was not ready to fight.

Adolf Hitler

b. April 20, 1889, d. April 30, 1945

Hitler was born in Austria. However, he fought in the German army during World War One and was awarded the Iron Cross, First Class for bravery. Hitler hated the Treaty of Versailles, which represented German humiliation after defeat in World War I. By 1920, he was a member of a right-wing party which came to be known as the Nazis. After an attempt to seize power in Germany in 1923, Hitler served a short prison sentence but then faded from the political scene until the economic crisis of 1929. Rocketing unemployment made people listen to the extreme messages of the Nazis. Hitler offered hope, pride, food and work to the German people. His ideas were outlined in his book Mein Kampf ('My Struggle') written during his imprisonment, in which he claimed Jews and Communists were the enemies of Germany. He promised to restore German power and claimed that the pure German people – whom he inaccurately described as 'Aryans' – were a master race who had a right to dominate Europe. By early 1933, Hitler had become Chancellor of Germany and a few months later he was its dictator.

In Germany, Hitler established a totalitarian dictatorship. The Nazi party was the only political party allowed. Through a combination of popular policies and fear, force and propaganda, Hitler and the Nazis established a stranglehold over Germany. During the 1930s, for 'good' Germans (ie those who supported the Nazis and fitted in with Nazi ideals) life seemed to get better with jobs, food and popular leisure activities all organised by the state. For those people the Nazis disapproved of, especially the Jews, life got worse. Secret police spied on the population and concentration camps were used to imprison any opposition. Nazi Germany was a Police State. The Nazis made the laws, enforced the laws and judged who was guilty or innocent.

The ideology of Nazism, created by Hitler, led to the Holocaust in which six million Jewish men, women and children were captured without trial, having committed no crimes; deported in cattle trains and held in concentration camps where they were starved, tortured and murdered. A further five million people: those with physical and mental disabilities, homosexuals, gypsies, political objectors and other opponents suffered as a result of Nazi ideology and were also abused and murdered.

Hitler's foreign policy was a combination of expansion and the uniting of all German-speaking people into a Greater Germany and aimed for the destruction of the Treaty of Versailles. Between 1935 and 1939, Hitler's breaking of treaty agreements and aggression was met with appeasement. Realising he was not going to meet forceful opposition, Hitler demanded, and got, more and more concessions from his former enemies, Britain and France. It was not until September 1939, when Nazi Germany invaded Poland, that Britain and France declared war on Germany, thereby starting World War Two. The war ended in 1945, just days after Hitler committed suicide in the ruins of Berlin.